The
Self-Hypnosis
Diet

The
Self-Hypnosis
Diet

*Use the Power of Your Mind to
Reach Your Perfect Weight*

**STEVEN GURGEVICH, Ph.D. &
JOY GURGEVICH**

SOUNDS TRUE
awakening wisdom

Sounds True, Inc., Boulder CO 80306
© 2007 Dr. Steven Gurgevich and Joy Gurgevich

Book Design: Chad Morgan

Published 2007
Printed in Canada

ISBN-10: 1-59179-475-7
ISBN-13: 978-1-59179-475-2

Grateful acknowledgment is made to Ellyn Satter for permission to reprint on
page 159 an excerpt from *Secrets of Feeding a Healthy Family* (Madison, WI:
Kelcy Press, 1999).

Library of Congress Cataloging-in-Publication Data

Gurgevich, Steven.
The self-hypnosis diet : use the power of your mind to reach your perfect
weight / Steven Gurgevich and Joy Gurgevich.
     p. cm.
Includes bibliographical references.
ISBN-13: 978-1-59179-475-2
ISBN-10: 1-59179-475-7
1. Weight loss. 2. Mind and body. I. Gurgevich, Joy. II. Title.

RM222.2.G82 2007
615.8'5122--dc22

2006024816

CONTENTS

Foreword by Andrew Weil, M.D. ... 1

Introduction ... 5

A Note on Using the CD and Book ... 8

    1. The Magnificent Mind-Body Connection ... 11

    2. Believe You Can and You Will ... 31

    3. Simply Practicing Hypnosis ... 47

    4. Perfect Mind—Perfect Weight ... 59

    5. Love, Love Me Do ... 77

    6. Feeding Feeling ... 95

    7. Nourishing Your Love Affair with Food ... 119

    8. Clearing the Path to Your Perfect Weight ... 139

    9. Taking Care of You—Exploring Wholesome Foods and Other Wise Choices ... 169

  10. Now You Have It ... 199

Appendix A: Answers to Chapter 1 Quiz ... 207

Appendix B: The History of Hypnosis Timeline ... 211

Further Reading and Resources ... 215

About the Authors ... 223

FOREWORD

With an epidemic of obesity facing Americans today, it is vital to return our country to good health. Throughout my years of exploring alternatives to allopathic medicine, I have seen time and time again how significantly medical hypnosis can impact our health by allowing us to tap into our subconscious minds. Steven Gurgevich, Ph.D., and Joy Kettler Gurgevich are friends and colleagues I have known for many years. We work together at the Program in Integrative Medicine that I direct at the University of Arizona College of Medicine. Now they have combined their unique and masterful skills in medical hypnosis and behavioral nutrition to show people how to achieve a healthy lifestyle and maintain healthy weight. And it all begins by accessing the potential of the subconscious mind.

Life in America today is not so conducive to these goals. The vast majority of Americans are dependent upon the automobile for transport to work, school, and shopping. This discourages "built-in" physical activity that helps maintain normal weight. In Japan, China, and much of Europe, people still walk or bike to work and buy fresh, high-quality foods from shops within walking distance. In contrast, the food that is cheapest and most accessible in America is also the least nourishing. The combination of minimal physical activity and unwholesome foods has led our nation to its present epidemic of obesity. More than 65 percent of Americans are overweight and 30 percent are obese.

I believe the key to abating this epidemic is to begin grassroots education that encourages people to take personal responsibility for their good health and well-being. The ideas and suggestions introduced by the Gurgeviches in *The Self-Hypnosis Diet* are exactly what is needed to turn the tide.

When I was in medical school, I realized the importance of nutrition and exercise to good health, and in my work with patients and through the books I write, I try to share this knowledge with others. It is a pleasure to work with colleagues like Steve and Joy, who integrate and expand upon my ideas through their respective areas of expertise to lead others to success.

This book is different from all other weight loss books because it focuses on the power of the mind to create a lifestyle that normalizes weight. *The Self-Hypnosis Diet* covers all the influences that cause weight-gaining behaviors to develop. These include family patterns in childhood, emotional triggers for eating and weight gain, and obstacles inherent in each person, such as taste preferences, an inclination toward physical activity, willpower, self-love, and confidence. The artful use of the power of belief and the mind-body connection is woven with positive hypnotic suggestions on the accompanying trancework CD to reveal and undo patterns learned in the past.

You will find suggestions in the trancework to replace past patterns with lifestyle choices that promote healthy weight and manage hunger effectively. These use the subconscious mind's ability to accept what is imagined as real, greatly lessening the perceived stress of changing to healthier habits.

An important feature of *The Self-Hypnosis Diet* is the use of self-hypnosis to facilitate changes in behavior and attitude that *let you seemingly eat what you want and keep your perfect weight.* By creating the healthy lifestyle outlined in these pages and the trancework, you will discover that you are eating what you want and maintaining a healthy weight. This is because you have mindfully chosen to replace unwholesome foods and weight-gaining behaviors with moderate portions of nourishing foods and physical activities that keep your body vibrant. The mental sense that "you can eat without restriction or dieting" powerful-ly reinforces your commitment and motivation without causing feelings of lack or deprivation.

Overweight and obesity create many health risks. It is im-portant to remember that obesity is totally treatable. The remedy will not be found in the quick fix of a fad diet or magic sup-plement. Instead it involves enduring habits of wise nutritional choices and physical activity.

The Self-Hypnosis Diet is not a "diet" at all. The Gurgeviches recommend *not* being a dieter or "restricted eater." They base this recommendation on research that has conclusively shown dieting to be less effective for weight loss than changing behav-iors to achieve health.

People have difficulty losing weight because it requires changing habits and behaviors. Making long-standing dietary changes may create internal discomfort, because old habits cling and usually resist change. The Gurgeviches supply the ingredi-ent missing from most other diets and weight loss methods: the power of your mind to make changes more comfortable and effective. *The Self-Hypnosis Diet* combines the mind-body ap-proach of hypnosis with techniques of behavioral nutrition to overcome resistance so that you can more rapidly establish the lifestyle that maintains the weight you want.

The Gurgeviches say that these methods will work for you because they work for them. They work for me also. We are mindful about making wise nutritional choices and exercising regularly in what has become our permanent lifestyle. You can learn to do the same. By creating positive lifelong habits, you can take your mind off dieting and begin to enjoy the healthy weight this lifestyle promotes.

Andrew Weil, M.D.
Tucson, Arizona
June 2006

INTRODUCTION

Without leaps of imagination, or dreaming, we lose the excitement
of possibilities. Dreaming, after all, is a form of planning.
GLORIA STEINEM

When we were very young children, most of us played our days away, absorbing the bits and pieces of the world around us. We sang songs, danced, rode bicycles, were enchanted by our favorite stories, and delighted in our favorite foods. We all have memories of aromas wafting through the air, pulling us away from our play, tempting us briefly back into the kitchen, a reminder of our hunger. We dreamed at night and pretended by day, playing make-believe games of castles and kings, when everything was perfect and we were the stars of the show. That is what most of us did when we were very young children.

Then we grew up. Now, it seems as though the world is absorbing us and our childish delight in food is plagued by guilt or frenzied schedules, or just disinterest. Our youthful play has turned into frantic driving, endless e-mails, and plasma screen addiction. Our weekends, at best, promise a walk or maybe an hour at the local fitness center. The strong, energetic bodies of our youth are laden with pounds and more pounds of exhausting extra weight.

The Self-Hypnosis Diet is about playing and pretending again, relearning the delights of our youth, and peeling off the tiring extra weight once and for all. Within the chapters of this book, you will learn about the mind-body connection and self-hypnosis, and how they can be utilized to create the energetic body you want, the healthy body hidden inside. You will learn how pretending, which is the simple word for self-hypnosis, can turn your wishes into reality, and you can once again become the star of your show.

The Self-Hypnosis Diet does not impose a diet on you. Instead, it provides the *missing* ingredient in other diets. It addresses the role and power of your mind to make any diet or lifestyle change more effective. Our emphasis will be on guiding your hypnosis to help you maintain healthy thoughts, emotions, and beliefs, which assure healthy eating patterns and healthy living patterns. *The Self-Hypnosis Diet* is about focusing mental energy to achieve your healthy weight, much as a magnifying glass focuses sunlight. You might view this as a diet of mental energy that nourishes your motivation and beliefs to create your desired weight.

The Self-Hypnosis Diet is born of our years of counseling people to help them restore their healthy weight. Many of them had lost and regained hundreds of pounds, plodding unsuccessfully from one diet to another, constantly weighed down by the dismal prospects of feeling hungry and deprived. There seemed to be a missing ingredient for all these people. Most of them knew the "energy in/energy out" concept. Yet something doomed them to reverting to poor eating behaviors and food choices, even after significant weight loss. We knew that understanding the magnificent mind-body connection and learning to use the power of the subconscious mind would reveal the missing ingredient and create the breakthrough that people need to restore their healthy weight forever.

So, we invite you to enjoy your first taste of self-hypnosis. We are delighted with your intent and we are confident that you will learn to use the magnificent mind–body connection to restore the weight that is perfect for you.

Dr. G. and Joy

A Note on Using the CD and Book

The CD enclosed at the back of the book includes the self-hypnosis trancework that you will listen to and practice with while reading *The Self-Hypnosis Diet*. The trancework must be practiced in a safe environment, so *never* listen while you are driving a car or operating any type of machinery. Choose a regular time to practice your hypnosis every day. As with any new skill, regular practice improves results. Many people prefer to practice in the evening before going to sleep. We enjoy practicing our trancework without headphones, so the words "fill up the room." When the trancework is finished, we can begin a restful slumber. Choose a comfortable place where you do not have to pay attention to anything else. Sit in a chair, recline, or even lie down. Relax. Then, simply listen.

As you become familiar with the various trancework tracks, you will find that some contain images, suggestions, and ideas that resonate more for you than other parts of the trancework. Select the trancework that appeals to your unique needs.

You want to nourish your mind-body (subconscious) often with all the words, thoughts, and ideas that support your perfect weight. After you have read the entire book, we suggest you go back to it daily, open to any page, and read for a few minutes. Follow with your self-hypnosis trancework practice. An easy way to make this happen is to keep the book where you practice your trancework, so that you can read a few pages before your practice. Our book contains an array of ingredients. As you thumb through the pages, you will notice boxes sprinkled throughout the chapters. Some contain definitions and quotations. Others contain tips and techniques—what we call "Belief Boosters" and "Motivations Makers." Indulge yourself in all of the ideas. Choose your favorites. Select the parts that seem especially enticing or appropriate for you. Sample a few ideas that seem intriguing. You do not have to digest the entirety of this book. Perhaps just one "piece" will be the powerful catalyst to effect weight loss for you.

We do have a few words of direct guidance. The first three chapters are rich with information about the mind-body connection, the power of belief, and the practice of self-hypnosis. We recommend that you read the first three chapters *before* listening to the trancework on the CD. Those chapters will provide you with an excellent foundation, especially if this is your first experience with self-hypnosis. A directive near the end of chapter 3 indicates when to listen to the initial track of trancework.

CHAPTER 1

THE MAGNIFICENT MIND-BODY CONNECTION

*Human beings, by changing the inner attitudes of
their minds, can change the outer aspects of their lives.*
WILLIAM JAMES

O nce upon a time it was believed that the mind and
the body were distinct and separate from each other.
The seventeenth-century philosopher René Descartes
is credited with proclaiming this distinction. But he later said
that it was spoken only out of his love of the Church and that
he did not want to intrude on *matters of the heart,* for at that time
they were the considered to be the Church's domain. However, science and research have repeatedly shown that mind and
body are not two distinctly separate entities, but that they are
intricately connected. Mind and body cannot exist without the
presence of each other. One of the most important features of
the mind-body connection is that they are in constant communication, each influencing the other. You might think of your
mind and body as always speaking to each other. This is the
mind-body connection. Every thought and idea in your mind
has an effect on your body; and every sensation in your body has
an effect on your mind.

This book is about how your mind can influence your body for the better, to help you achieve the weight you were meant to have through the practice of self-hypnosis. Before jumping into the actual methods that will lead you to your perfect body weight, we would like to talk about hypnosis, its origins, and what it actually is in order to separate some fact from fiction. We would also like to introduce what we believe is at the heart of the concept of hypnosis—the mind-body connection. Understanding this intimate communication within your body will help you use self-hypnosis to ultimately achieve your perfect weight.

It is important to understand that thoughts are things. You cannot see them, but you know you have them. You may not feel every thought, but if you had biofeedback sensors attached to your body, you would see the instantaneous changes in your body created by your thoughts, positively or negatively. For example, if you were to think of someone who makes you angry, you would see immediate changes in heart function, blood vessel dilation or constriction, changes within your nervous system, and muscle tension. All these physical changes would happen because of a single thought. What this tells us is that your thoughts and ideas are chemically transmitted to the rest of your body, such that your body is "thinking" the same thing you are putting in your mind, but in your body's own way, with its own physiological responses. Sometimes you are aware of your body's response to what you think. Most of the time you are not aware that it is sharing the experience of your thoughts. The manner in which your body responds to the experience is based upon many factors, including your personality, past experiences, and learned patterns of response. With the repetition of these patterns, your body becomes programmed to perform in a certain way. It learns or becomes conditioned to that response pattern. The good news is that anything that your body has learned can be unlearned by creating a different response. Self-hypnosis is a very powerful and effective tool to help you unlearn old patterns and replace them with more desirable patterns.

> *You never can tell what your thoughts will do*
> *In bringing you hate or love,*
> *For thoughts are things, and their airy wings*
> *Are swifter than carrier doves.*
> *They follow the law of the Universe,*
> *Each thing must create its kind,*
> *And they speed o'er the track to bring you back*
> *Whatever went out from your mind.*
> ELLA WHEELER WILCOX, "You Can Never Tell"

Just as your thoughts influence your body, your body influences your thoughts. There are times when you feel a sensation in your body, such as hunger or thirst, that causes you to feel an emotion or think a thought or have an idea in mind. If your mouth feels dry, you probably have a thought to drink water. But sometimes there is confusion—for example, when a feeling of being emotionally hurt might be confused with a sensation of "I need to eat" or "I want to eat." These are some of the dynamics that we will be exploring and addressing within *The Self-Hypnosis Diet*.

Adopt the idea of having a "mind-body" which is the exquisite connection that mind and body share. Think of your subconscious mind as the "mind of your body," your "mind-body." Instead of thinking that mind and body are distinct, use the terms "mind-body," "mind of your body," and "subconscious mind" as all representing the same thing. We will be using these terms interchangeably, but all three represent the same concept.

MIND-BODY CONNECTION The complex of intricate interactions and responses among mental, emotional, and physical aspects of one's mind and body. It refers to the functional dualism that mind and body are intricately connected in a web of constant interaction such that the idea of "mind" and "body" may be viewed as "mind-body."

IN THEIR OWN WORDS ...

My food choices are so much healthier, I don't even want or desire foods that are not nourishing or beneficial. My energy level has increased and I'm walking at least one mile a day. I have always believed there was a mind–body connection and the *Lose Weight with Hypnosis* CDs have made me more of a believer. I don't even have to consciously think about what I should be eating or doing, it just comes naturally. These CDs have made a difference in my life.

JONATHAN

What Hypnosis *Is*

Self-hypnosis is a very effective way for you to talk directly to the mind of your body (the subconscious mind or mind–body). It provides you with a way to remove any obstacles and confusion within the dialogue of your mind–body, so that mind–body is sharing exactly what you want in a way that creates your healthy weight and healthy lifestyle. Before we go any further, we would like you to complete a short mental exercise that will help you begin learning about the power and the simplicity of self-hypnosis. Below are ten "true or false" statements about hypnosis. Read the statements and wonder, guess, or decide "true or false" according to what you *currently believe* about hypnosis.

What Do You Now Believe About Hypnosis?

1. Hypnosis is complicated and takes many sessions and much instruction.
2. To experience hypnosis, you must be hypnotized by someone who knows how to do it to you.
3. When experiencing a hypnotic trance, one loses consciousness.

4. The subconscious mind cannot tell the difference between what is real and what is imagined.

5. Hypnosis can make you do things that are against your will or violate your values.

6. Most people go into trance every day.

7. All hypnosis is self-hypnosis.

8. Hypnosis can help your body heal wounds faster.

9. Your body has a language of its own.

10. You can use hypnosis to influence your physical responses like digestion, breathing, etc.

11. Stage hypnosis is the same as medical hypnosis.

12. Sometimes you are not even aware that you are already in a trance.

13. Hypnosis is a purely mental or psychological phenomenon—it is "all in the mind."

14. There are some people who cannot be hypnotized.

15. With hypnosis you can give messages to your body and your body can give messages to you.

16. There are thousands of published research studies and articles that demonstrate the benefits and effectiveness of hypnosis.

Reading these statements is an important step. It primes your conscious mind to be on the alert for the answers throughout these pages and your experience with the audio CD. (If you can't wait, the answers are in Appendix A.)

It is important to answer thoroughly any questions you may have about hypnosis. The reason for this is simple. To be able to "let go" of any hesitations and experience hypnosis, you must feel safe and comfortable within yourself when using the techniques presented on the CD portion of *The Self-Hypnosis Diet*. The more you know about hypnosis, the more comfortable and confident you will feel using it.

Hypnosis Defined

Below is the formal definition of hypnosis from a major professional association, as well as Dr. G.'s own definition. You will see that they speak about it in a similar fashion.

ASCH (American Society of Clinical Hypnosis)

Hypnosis is a state of inner absorption, concentration, and focused attention. It is like using a magnifying glass to focus the rays of the sun and make them more powerful. Similarly, when our minds are concentrated and focused, we are able to use our minds more powerfully. Because hypnosis allows people to use more of their potential, learning self-hypnosis is the ultimate act of self-control.

Dr. Steven Gurgevich's Definition

Hypnosis is a system or collection of methods that enable mind and body to share information more effectively. One of those methods is called trance. It is a process of creating an inner-self experience of focused consciousness that enables your mind and body to accept and share your intentions, beliefs, and expectations as true. The focused intention of your consciousness magnifies your power of belief (and the capacity of your belief) to cause your subconscious mind to accept and act upon intention.

Applications of Hypnosis

Studies show that hypnosis is an effective tool for accessing the mind-body connection. *The Self-Hypnosis Diet* will show you how to use self-hypnosis and access your mind-body connection for successful weight loss.

BELIEF BOOSTER

Hypnosis can actually help you lose weight.

HARVARD MEDICAL SCHOOL PSYCHOTHERAPIST JEAN FAIN,
O: The Oprah Magazine, August 2004

Clinical and medical applications of hypnosis are plentiful. As many of our clients have done, you may use hypnosis to:

- change habits and behaviors such as smoking, nail biting, or hair pulling
- treat anxiety disorders or phobias, like the fear of flying or fear of heights
- uncover subconscious emotional conflicts or dynamics that underlie a variety of symptoms
- relieve pain
- provide anesthesia during surgery
- help wounds heal faster
- heal skin conditions
- heal irritable bowel syndrome
- provide relief for allergies
- promote the healing of asthma
- suppress or enhance the immune system
- address countless other applications, including expediting weight loss

Not only are these methods useful with adults, but children can benefit greatly and there are limitless pediatric applications. This is due, in part, to the fact that children are outstanding hypnotic subjects. They are wonderfully imaginative and have a great ability to pretend. When we work with children, we do not use the terms

TRANCE
A conscious state of focused attention and absorption in one's ideas, thoughts, and images, with a narrowing of awareness to other stimuli, which enhances the acceptance of suggestion and the response by the subconscious mind.

TRANCEWORK
The activity of using hypnotic trance to achieve a benefit or therapeutic outcome.

HYPNOTHERAPY
Hypnosis used within psychotherapy or medical interventions.

HYPNOTIC
SUGGESTION
A statement
offered during
trance that
either directly or
indirectly conveys
the message of
what you want
your subconscious
to act upon or
bring about.

"hypnosis" or "trance." Instead we call it "imaginative medicine" and they are asked to simply "pretend." The myriad applications for pediatric hypnosis include enuresis (bedwetting), thumb sucking, nail biting, hair pulling, low self-esteem, anxiety, pain control, bleeding control for hemophiliacs, nausea, ease of emergency room procedures, preoperative comfort, induction of anesthesia, postoperative comfort, and grief and mourning.

Let us just say that hypnosis is a collection of methods that allow your mind-body to share information more effectively. More specifically, hypnosis is a way for you to provide your mind-body with suggestions, thoughts, ideas, and images that effectively remove any obstacles to weight loss and enhance or maintain your perfect weight.

BELIEF BOOSTER

Imagine that when you eat, you feel satisfied sooner and therefore lose weight more rapidly. Imagine that the pain after heart-bypass or dental surgery feels merely like mild pressure. Imagine that your skin rash is clearing up. Recent clinical studies suggest that hypnosis ... can indeed help motivated people accomplish those health goals.

CONSUMER REPORTS ON HEALTH, February 2004

Trance and Daydreaming

Everyday experiences of trance are common. When you are staring out a window, your eyes are open. They are recording light and shape and color. The rods and cones in your eyes are responding, and the optic nerve carries the information to your brain. You are staring off into space. You are technically "seeing," but you are not necessarily "looking" at what you are seeing. This is an example of an everyday experience of trance.

You can also stare with your ears. Eardrums are tympanic. They are like the heads on drums. They move with the changes in air pressure (sound waves). When you are staring with your ears, you are technically "hearing" because your eardrum is moving and the tiny bones in the ear carry the message along the nerve pathways to the brain, but you are not "listening." You can be "seeing" but not "looking." You can be "hearing" but not "listening." You are more absorbed in yourself, in your thoughts and ideas, than in the environment outside of you. This state of focused concentration, which is just like a daydream, is an everyday or natural hypnotic trance.

Another example of an everyday trance might include being so absorbed in a book that you are not paying much attention to what is going on around you. Or, you can be absorbed in a movie, and sometime during that movie, you might actually get excited or frightened or emotionally involved in the experience of what you are seeing and hearing. In these times of being so absorbed in your experience of daydreaming, reading, watching a movie, or listening to music, your thoughts—and the feelings created by your thoughts—become "real"... or seem to be at the time. When this happens, your mind-body or subconscious cannot tell the difference. Your heart rate may speed up or slow down, muscles may tighten or relax, and you might become hungry, thirsty, or nauseous. In other words, your mind and body share the experience so well together that it becomes a very real physical experience. Those are everyday trances. As you can see, there is no going out, there is no going under. At all times, you are in control and you are aware that you are in control. If you think of a hypnotic trance in the same way as a daydream, you will have a better feel for just what it is and what it is not.

What Hypnosis Is *Not*

The word "hypnosis" may conjure up misconceptions that leave a bad taste in our mouths. This is due mostly to the advent of stage hypnotists (see definition of stage hypnosis on page 21). One misconception about hypnosis is that it is "done to" someone or that a person "gets hypnotized." This is totally false. No one hypnotizes another person. A good therapist or clinician only facilitates helping people learn to do this, much as they would learn to do meditation.

Loss of consciousness is another misconception. You do not lose consciousness when "in trance" doing hypnosis. At all times you are fully aware of where you are and what you are doing. The hypnotic trance itself is similar to what you experience when you are in a daydream, when you are wonderfully absorbed in your own thoughts and ideas.

Another misconception about hypnosis is the surrendering of your will. At all times you are in control and will not do anything against your will or your best interest. This includes revealing secrets or embarrassing yourself. You will not do anything in trance that you would not do in a regular waking state.

Some people have the false idea that they may not be able to come out of trance. But everyone comes out of trance because they put themselves into it. Hypnosis can naturally lead to falling asleep, which is a way of coming out of trance because sleep is not hypnosis. The difference between sleep and hypnosis is that during sleep you are not conscious. A hypnotic trance is a waking state in which you are absorbed in your own thoughts and ideas so thoroughly that you are ignoring the stimuli from the environment around you or within you.

Remember, with hypnosis you are in control of choosing what you want your mind-body to share. You can choose what and how to respond. A part of your body may itch but you can choose not to scratch it. The phone may ring and you can decide you do not need to answer it. Becoming absorbed in your thoughts and ideas is the gentle journey of going into the center of yourself that we refer to as "going into trance." We might also say, "Let yourself daydream," or to a child we might just say, "Pretend."

Because a trance state is a passive or relaxed form of concentration or self-absorption, you will make it happen by feeling comfortable enough to let it happen. To be comfortable you must feel safe. That is why it is important to answer the true/false questions about what hypnosis really is and what it really is not. Clarifying any misconceptions allows you to see with fresh eyes that *everything you need is already within you.*

A Short History of Hypnosis

Hypnosis is not a new practice. Although its history dates back to over four thousand years ago, it only became known as "hypnosis" in the last 150 years. History shows mind–body methods of healing in ancient China, Egypt, and Greece. From the sleep and healing temples of ancient Greece to Franz Mesmer's magnetic passes in France in the late 1700s, mind–body methods of healing are examples of medical applications that use the mind–body connection. Although Mesmer was discredited by a royal commission headed by Benjamin Franklin, his records and patients depicted greater success than did his contemporaries. In the mid- to late 1800s, English and French physicians took an interest in the results Mesmer had achieved using methods like magnetic passes. James Braid and James Esdale, two Scottish surgeons, felt that Mesmer's success was entirely due to suggestion. A French physician coined the term "hypnosis" after Hypnos, the god of sleep. The rekindled interest in methods of suggestion or hypnosis led to hundreds of documented cases of surgery and other procedures done entirely with hypnosis as anesthesia. Dr. John Elliotson published the *Zoist,* the first professional journal devoted to medical applications of hypnosis. But the popular or lay movement proliferated, with many "healers" professing

STAGE HYPNOSIS Stage hypnosis uses methods of influence and hypnosis exclusively for entertainment purposes. That is, the show is a performance to entertain an audience. Oftentimes, illusion and other factors best explain what the audience sees when a stage hypnotist uses a combination of behavioral techniques with willing volunteers who agree to be "part of the show."

to use "mind cures." Some were done as sideshows and others were done by well-meaning persons. However, the medical profession distanced itself from the unregulated "lay" hypnotists in much the same way professional hypnotists today turn away from being associated with stage hypnotists.

Another factor that diminished the spark of hypnosis in the 1800s was the advent of chemical anesthesia, ether. Despite the forces that diminished the proliferation of hypnosis in medicine, the results obtained with hypnosis were both consistent and impressive. During both world wars, army physicians used hypnosis successfully to help soldiers cope with pain when medical supplies were exhausted, and address battle fatigue, anxiety, and fear—so much so that a group of physicians formed the Society for Clinical and Experimental Hypnosis in 1949. In 1955 and 1958, respectively, the British Medical Association and the American Medical Association adopted hypnosis as valid within medical education curriculum. In 1957 the American Society of Clinical Hypnosis (ASCH) was founded by Dr. Milton Erickson and others to further promote professional training in applications of hypnosis.

In the last fifty years, thousands of studies have been conducted that continue to demonstrate, and expand the usefulness of, this mind-body method. For information about professional associations, see Further Reading and Resources at the back of the book.

Speaking the Language of the Mind-Body

Words are powerful. They are the verbal expression of thoughts and ideas. Your subconscious mind hears everything you hear, everything you say, and everything that you picture, image, or pretend. But most importantly, your subconscious mind interprets these words and thoughts in its own language, which is not quite the same language that you consciously think or speak. Your subconscious mind, your mind-body, takes everything literally. Consciously, you think both figuratively and literally; you can use figures of speech and know what you mean. For example, you might say, "I want to lose weight so badly." You know what you mean, but the subconscious mind hears something else and responds to what it hears. *For the moment let yourself imagine the subconscious as a waiter or waitress within your mind-body, taking your order.* The literal understanding of what was said is, "I want to lose weight ..." The subconscious mind then asks, "And how would you like it done?" "... so badly." And that is how it is done subconsciously: badly. When offering yourself suggestions, you want to be mindful of the "literal" interpretation of the words you use. That is the beauty of using pictures and images in imagination: they are already in a literal form, and there is no confusion as to what you want.

Don't worry about having to learn a new language to communicate with your mind-body. That is our job, and the trancework sessions on the CD were specifically created to do this for you.

> Words are ... the most powerful drugs known to mankind.
> RUDYARD KIPLING

"Try" Does Not Mean "Do"

We all use the word "try" in our speech, and we know what we mean when we use it. But look at what your subconscious mind does with "try." Remember, the subconscious interprets everything literally. So, what is a "try"? We cannot perceive a literal "try," for it is only a figure of speech. A "try" does not take up space or have weight, so it is not literally there; it is only a concept we use. Trying to remember is not the same as remembering. Trying to fall asleep is not the same as going to sleep. Trying to do anything is not the same as doing it, because the outcome of "trying" can be success or failure. The subconscious translates "try" into a literal meaning of "to try" or "to put on trial," much like "trying a case" in court. The literal meaning is "to see whether or not." So, the outcome of "try" can be success or failure, yes or no, true or false. "Doing" is always successful and can be modified by many adjectives, such as rapidly, comfortably, poorly, easily, and so on. Notice how the literal message is diluted if you put a "try" in the following examples: "I am trying to lose weight" is not the same as "I am losing weight." "I am trying to exercise" is not the same as "I am doing more exercise." Become very sensitive to the word "try" and teach yourself to replace the word "try" with some type of "do." "I am losing weight." "I am taking a walk in the park tomorrow morning." Remember the advice Yoda gave to the young warrior Luke in *Star Wars*: "Do, or do not. There is no try."

> Do not try.
> Just do it.

"Never the Nots"

Émile Coué, a French psychologist, wrote a book in 1920 about self-hypnosis entitled *Self Mastery Through Conscious Autosuggestion*. He was perhaps the first doctor to remind us that we do not need anyone else to offer us hypnotic suggestion; we can do it for ourselves. He taught his patients "self-hypnosis" and advised them to daily speak the words, "Every day, in every way, I am getting better and better." He also advised, "Never the nots." When speaking affirmations to yourself, never use the word "not." The word "not" has no literal meaning to your subconscious mind (similar to "try"). You know what it means and you use it with ease in your conscious everyday speech. Remember, the subconscious only understands words on a literal level. For example, try *not* to think of a birthday cake. What image just came to mind—a pear, a Chevrolet, a giraffe? No, it was probably a frosted cake with lit candles. When you use a "not ... something" your subconscious mind only hears the "something." Remember Dr. Coue's advice,

"Never the nots." "I will stop eating when I feel full" instead of "I will not eat too much." "I will eat one piece of chocolate for dessert" instead of "I will not eat too much chocolate." "I will enjoy one serving of potatoes tonight" instead of "I will not eat too many potatoes tonight."

IN THEIR OWN WORDS ...

Self-hypnosis has definitely helped me. All my life I turned to food for comfort. Now, I have more control than ever before. I can be with a group of people who are eating, and I don't feel a need to eat. Everything used to revolve around food. Now, life is more interesting. The Magnificent Make-Over is really cool. I used to dread exercise and now I look forward to it. Before I started this program, I had high blood sugar, fatty liver, and thyroid dysfunction. Now, all my numbers are normal.

LORI

Metaphors: Powerful Messages to the Mind of Your Body

Metaphors are figures of speech that are useful to us when communicating with people. When we use metaphors, we understand what we are saying consciously, but often we are not fully aware of what our mind-body actually hears. We cannot iterate enough: the mind-body hears words literally and responds to the literal meaning. We need to tell you something very special and important to remember about your subconscious mind, the mind of your body. It cannot tell the difference between what is real and what you imagine. This is obvious when you consider being immersed in a good movie or novel; our bodies can react physically to something we imagine in the movie or novel, just as if it were really happening. Perhaps you have had this experience: You are walking along a sidewalk, a trail, or even on the carpet in your house and you jump out of the way of something that turns out to be harmless, a piece of string or a rubber band. But in the moment you jumped out of the way, there was a part of you that believed you needed to be jumped out of the way, even before you could think to do it. Since your subconscious mind could not tell the difference between what was a real or imagined threat, *it* jumped you out of the way to protect you in either case.

Here are a few more examples: "I just look at food and gain weight." "Ice cream goes right to my hips." "If I walk past a buffet of desserts, they seem to jump like magnets to my rear end." These are metaphors. When people make statements like these to themselves, to their mind–body, what are they programming their mind–body to do? Are they asking it to slow down their metabolism to actually fulfill the suggestion that looking at food causes them to gain weight? Will the mind–body make them perspire less, concentrate their urine, slow down the gut motility or grumbling in their stomachs? Remember, it hears words literally and does everything in its power to make them happen.

You may have heard other people say "I can eat anything and my weight stays the same." If they really believe that, are they programming their bodies to do everything to fulfill that belief and not gain weight? Are they asking the mind–body to speed up metabolism, perspire more, increase their intestinal motility, digestion, and elimination? Will the mind–body actually create a feeling of a greater sense of fullness much sooner? It hears these words literally, "I can eat anything and my weight stays the same."

The following are examples of how the metaphors we use are actually powerful messages to the mind of our body that we are unaware of. Think about what some of these metaphors might mean or how they might be expressed by your body.

- He's a pain in the neck (or much lower).
- She gets under my skin.
- That just burns me up.
- It's too hard to swallow.
- That just bugs the crap out of me.
- I will breathe easy when this is over.
- They just rub me the wrong way.
- It breaks my heart.
- I don't have a leg to stand on.
- I need to get something off my chest.
- What's too hard to look at?
- What's weighing you down?
- What are you "weighting/waiting" for?
- When you get big, you will …
- What is "weighing" on your mind?
- Have you had "more than your share"?
- I don't want to lose anymore.
- What are you "fed up" with?
- I want to be noticed.
- I want to throw my weight around.
- I'm no "lightweight." (Someone who feels they are not being taken seriously.)
- Are you too big for your britches?
- I want more space.
- I've been "weighting/waiting and weighting/waiting" for this to work.
- I don't fit in.
- What are you hungry for?
- I have a hunger I can't fill.
- Carrying the weight of responsibility for others …
- Food is love.
- Swallow your pride.
- I'm starving. I could eat a horse.

A Big Metaphor

When you were a child, many choices were withheld from you, but now you are an adult and have the freedom to make many choices. Let us look at this idea the way a child might experience it. The child sees something and wants it, and the feeling of wanting becomes overwhelming. The child asks the parent and becomes excited with wanting the thing desired. But the child cannot make it happen because the parent will choose what the parent wants to choose—or at least that is how it seems to the child. Perhaps you can remember what it felt like when you really wanted to have something and it was denied. The child experiences this denial as painful and upsetting. It hurts, and the child may cry or become very angry. He might come to believe, "When I am bigger, I can have whatever I want." Or the belief may happen as a result of being told, "When you are bigger you can choose what you want." Children do not have the intellectual sophistication to understand the way adults can. The belief that when they are bigger they can have what they want is a form of comfort to them. But it is also a double-edged sword, because what does their mind-body (subconscious) do with the words "big" and "bigger"? It treats them as literal and concrete. "Bigger" becomes associated with the comfort of being able to have their wants satisfied and the protection from that form of emotional pain. Now, as an adult, you know that the message was supposed to mean: "When you are older and wiser, you can make these choices for yourself." However, the subconscious of the child hears "big" and "bigger" and interprets the message literally and with all the emotional energy present when their wants are being denied. What gets programmed into the mind-body? The literal translation of "big" and "bigger" represents a big or bigger body. Your subconscious mind does not even distinguish between an adult body and a big adult body—the emphasis is only on "big."

For example, eight-year-old Annie went shopping with her mother and older sister for Easter dresses. Annie dissolved in tears when the dress she loved was not her size. Her older sister also loved the dress, and it fit her, so her mother bought it and told Annie, "When you are bigger you can wear the dress." During a session of hypnosis, the adult Annie was asked, "Is there any reason your body wants to hold on to excess weight?" She became disturbed and tears rolled down her cheeks as she recalled her mother saying, "Annie, you can wear the dress when you are bigger." Once this emotional obstacle was revealed, Annie was able to let go of her excess weight within a year.

The important lesson in examining these metaphors and phrases is to think about how the mind-body might act them out physically and literally. Remember, your subconscious mind cannot tell the difference between what is real and what you imagine.

That is why we are inviting you to stir your imagination and indulge in your childhood art of pretending. When you tell your mind-body what you want and what you imagine, in the language it understands, you will discover how that dialogue leads to your perfect weight and healthy lifestyle. You will truly appreciate the magnificent mind-body connection.

CHAPTER 2

BELIEVE YOU CAN
AND YOU WILL

In the province of the mind, what one believes
to be true either is true or becomes true ...
JOHN LILLY

The Essential Ingredients:
Motivation, Belief, and Expectation

You control the essential ingredients that make self-hypnosis work
for you. Actually, these are the same ingredients that create your
experience of success for any goal you choose. Let us look at each
element and how you may use it to perform for you.

Motivation

Motivation is the energy of your desire, of what you want.
Wanting is a feeling that you can control. For most of your life
you have mainly controlled your desire or wanting by limiting
it or denying it. You may be very good at controlling your
desires and wanting in some areas and weak or unpracticed
in others. Since this is a "diet" book, you may have already
prepared yourself to hear that this "diet" will be like the others that have told you what you must deny yourself or limit.

That is, the other diets have told you what *not to want* and the emphasis may have been about "not wanting" some foods that you have grown to love. Welcome to a new way of treating yourself; we will encourage you to get even better at "wanting." Denial is not included in *The Self-Hypnosis Diet*. Your motivation is a key factor, one of the basic and essential ingredients. We want you to focus your energy of *wanting* not toward food but toward the motivation that clearly tells your mind–body what you want it to create: perfect weight. We encourage you to get really good at wanting your perfect weight. Here is an example. Let us say that you are in a swimming pool and suddenly you breathe in a mouthful of water. In that moment you want only one thing, a breath of air. It feels like life or death, and a breath of air is the only thing on your mind at this time. The wanting is so intense and powerful that it overshadows all other thoughts and propels you to do whatever it takes to get that breath of air. That is how much we want you to want the weight and body image that you desire.

Belief and Believing

Beliefs are those thoughts and ideas that are true for you. They do not have to be scientifically proven for you to know them to be true for you. Whether you are aware of it or not, your actions, both conscious and subconscious, are based on your beliefs. Even though your beliefs are in the form of thoughts and ideas, they shape your experience by affecting your actions in life. If you believe that animals make good companions, you probably have a cat, or dog, or parrot, or a ferret or two. If you believe that coffee keeps you awake at night, you probably do not drink coffee before going to bed. The power of believing lets you influence your body in ways that might seem astounding. Placebo responses, where individuals respond to an inert substance as if it were the real

We have to formulate what we want, be so concentrated on it, so focused on it, and so aware of it that we lose track of ourselves, we lose track of time, we lose track of our identity. The moment we become so involved in the experience that we lose track of ourselves, we lose track of time, is the only picture that's real. Everybody's had the experience of making up their mind that they've wanted something. That's quantum physics in action. That's manifesting reality.

DR. JOSEPH DISPENZA, from *What the Bleep Do We Know!?*

THE SELF-HYPNOSIS DIET

medication, are common examples of how beliefs are experienced in the body. If a person really believes that he will get well when taking a certain medication, it will happen whether the tablet contains medication or is simply inert. In the same way, if a person really believes that he can achieve high grades in college, it will happen. If a person really believes that he can attain his perfect weight, it will happen.

Remember your make-believe games as a child. Your ability to pretend is just as strong now as when you were very young. It may be a little rusty and you may need a bit of practice, but when you allow yourself to pretend and let yourself believe in what you are pretending, you will discover a very powerful tool. You will discover that this is a wonderfully effective way to deliver your intentions, those messages of what you want, to all of the cells and tissues and organs of your body, which respond by bringing that intention into reality for you. We can't say this enough: thoughts are things. The thoughts, the pictures, the ideas you put in your mind become the messages your self-hypnosis conveys to your mind-body, ultimately turning your perfect body into a reality. Pretending is choosing what to believe and becoming absorbed in those ideas. Just as a magnifying glass can focus rays of sunlight, you can focus your mental energy to make your thoughts, ideas, and beliefs real for your body.

Believe in love. Believe in magic. Hell, believe in Santa Claus. Believe in others. Believe in yourself. Believe in your dreams. If you don't, who will?
JON BON JOVI

Expectation

You may not always get what you want, but you do get what you expect. Expectations contain the energy of beliefs, and become the results of what is believed. Here is an example of how to "expect." When you sat down to read this book, you did not examine the chair or sofa to test its ability to hold your weight. You just sat down without thinking about it. You did not have to think about it, because a part of you is confident, and has so much faith in the chair, that you just "expected" it to hold you. That is how to expect the perfect body weight you desire. Keeping this in mind, be mindful of what you say to yourself and others regarding your body weight expectations. "I always gain weight over the holidays." "Last night I ate two pieces of cake, and this morning I was two pounds heavier."

MOTIVATION MAKER

A person must consume an extra 3,500 calories *above* what the body burns in order to gain one pound of fat. Splurging on an occasional wedge of pecan pie is not going to have a devastating effect on anyone's weight loss plan.

Mind-Body in Focus

Each of the essential ingredients can produce powerful results when focused within the mind-body. However, when these ingredients are aligned properly within the process of self-hypnosis, their effectiveness is magnified a hundredfold. Self-hypnosis is a process for creating your reality. You might think this sounds magical or too good to be true, but that is relative to what you have experienced up to this point in your life. These ideas may be very new to you. Here is an example of the "relative" nature of new ideas. Imagine that you are given a private jet airplane which is beautifully outfitted with luxurious appointments and a well-trained crew. It is a wonderful gift and you get to show this engineering marvel to some individuals who have never seen anything like it. Let us say that your pilot flies you back in time to just before December 17, 1903, when the Wright brothers announced their first flight at Kitty Hawk. You are eager to show this wonder of engineering to the Wright brothers, who come to greet you. What might happen? Perhaps they would be scared, and wouldn't believe that it is possible to fly in a metal bird. You could offer them a ride and they might choose to run from you. People can resist or reject new ideas, even when they are wonderful. The philosopher Arthur Schopenhauer said, "Every man takes the limits of his own field of vision for the limits of the world." Stretch your view and allow yourself the opportunity to become familiar with the ideas of self-hypnosis.

In *The Self-Hypnosis Diet,* we are offering you ideas that may stretch your imagination and shrink your clothing size. To say that self-hypnosis is a process by which you create your reality may seem too good to be true or even unbelievable right now, maybe as fantastic as a time machine is for some. That is fine, for right now; but open your mind and imagination to the possibilities that this gives you to attain your perfect body weight. Let yourself believe that this process is real and true, because it is, and because it relies upon your *belief* to become true.

Your subconscious (mind-body) uses the combination of what you want (motivation), what you believe, and what you expect as a blueprint for action. The results are achieved by your mind-body (subconscious), and not by thinking or analyzing. If a person touches a cold surface that she believes is very hot, she can produce a blister or burn response. Conversely, a person touching a very hot surface thinking that it is cool may not produce a burn response. People who walk over hot coals while imagining that they are cool may experience a thermal injury (some minor scorching on the soles of their feet), but their immune system does not respond with a burn (blistering, pain, etc.) because their minds tell their bodies how to react. Again, it is the alignment of all three of the essential ingredients that makes this possible:

- wanting to do it
- believing it possible
- expecting to be successful

This is the key to success. Your body carries out your beliefs. Your beliefs direct your actions, which in turn shape your experience.

Some describe this process as creating your success or creating your experience in life. In our culture, we see this described within the motivational and positive mental attitude literature. It can be seen in many areas of metaphysics. You can also look back to the ancients and see it described in the terms of the historical period. A person much wiser than we are said, "It will be done unto you according to your belief." In the present age of integrative medicine and psychology, we call it self-hypnosis or mind-body medicine. There are now numerous scientific studies that demonstrate amazing results for pain control, wound healing, physical alteration, and many more health benefits than we previously thought possible.

Choosing Your Beliefs

You have the ability to choose your beliefs. You may choose to believe what you see, in the sense of "See it to believe it" or "Seeing is believing." This is pretty easy to do. You experience something with your senses, and that is a familiar way of choosing whether it is believable or not. But you may also choose to believe it first and then see it, which may require some practice. Most people find it easier to let the world tell them what is true or what to believe. The television, media, newspapers, books, teachers, and experts bombard us with what to believe. You grew up learning about the world and yourself from many external sources. This led to a familiar pattern of observing and receiving information about the world from outside yourself, and you chose which information to make a part of your belief system. This included beliefs about your body. For example, when your stomach makes a rumbling sound, you believe that means you are hungry. Or you feel nauseous and believe you are sick. Both of these are examples of observed events: you observed a connection once and chose to believe it.

In *The Self-Hypnosis Diet,* we are proposing that you turn that practice around with this idea: "Believe it and you will see it." This means that you first choose what to believe and then your body acts upon it as true and makes it real in your experience. One of the important messages we hope you will receive from this book is that your mind-body hears everything you hear, everything you say, everything you think, picture, or imagine in your mind, and it cannot tell the difference between what is real and what you imagine. It acts upon what you want, believe, and expect. With this in mind, which of these statements would help you experience the perfect weight you desire: "I just look at food and gain weight" or "I can eat anything and my weight stays the same"? Surely the latter. But which statement do you personally *believe to be true* for you? Again, it will be done unto you according to your belief. We will help you with the ideas, language, and images that formulate effective hypnotic suggestions, but you have total control over what you choose to believe.

As you read the ideas in this book and hear the hypnotic suggestions offered during the trancework on the CD, you will make many choices for yourself. We wholeheartedly encourage you to choose to *believe it so you will see it* for yourself. Your subconscious (mind-body) cannot tell the difference, and will act on what you select either way. Why not select what you *really* want?

The Energy of Emotions

Not all thoughts and beliefs manifest themselves into your experience. Only those that have the *energy* of your feelings (emotions), along with your belief and your expectation that something is going to happen, will manifest themselves. Your feelings or emotions are a form of energy that influences this process of creation. That is, when you have a strong feeling about a belief, it contains energy. That energy creates your experience and further reinforces your beliefs and expectations. We are talking about the combined energy of your thoughts, your beliefs, your expectations, and what you want. The mental energy behind what you want and how much you let yourself want it creates motivation. So perhaps you can see that it is important to let yourself *truly want* something with great feeling. If you combine *feeling* with *want,* you empower the process you are setting into motion within you.

Make sure that your feelings remain positive. You can determine when they are positive or negative by how they make you feel. It's simple. Emotions that make you feel good are positive and emotions that make you feel bad are negative. Keep all of these energies positive by feeling good about your wanting (desire), beliefs, and expectations. If you have negative thoughts and emotions, they will damage your motivation. If you have positive thoughts and emotions, they will reinforce your motivation. Thoughts, beliefs, and expectations are equal-opportunity energies. You can attract them and produce positive or negative effects and outcomes. If you are negative, expect negative results. If you are positive, expect positive results. In this manner any thought, belief, or expectation produces a negative or positive result. It's a no-brainer—if you want success, seek positive energy from positive thoughts and feelings.

Charles spoke a litany of negative words. "My work is overwhelming. I have no time to do anything but climb out of bed in the morning, drive to the office, and try to keep everybody happy. I get a headache just thinking about my life. I can't possibly think about losing weight—it's not in the picture." Guess what? Charles gets headaches all the time, and he continues to gain weight; and he will do this until he stops using negative words to describe his life.

> One ship drives east and another drives west,
> With the self-same winds that blow,
> 'Tis the set of the sails
> And not the gales
> That tell them the way they go.
> ELLA WHEELER WILCOX

Choosing Your Feelings

Your mind-body also perceives your belief based on your underlying feeling. Here is an example. Let us say that you want to believe something that will help you achieve your goal. You compose an affirmation and begin saying it aloud to yourself. Affirmations are a wonderful way to create positive ideas and beliefs. Speaking affirmations allows your ears to hear your voice speak them. This too is a way of choosing your beliefs and reinforcing them. For example, you may say the affirmation, "I am lighter and thinner today." But what do you feel? If you "feel" you are overweight or feel that the affirmation is untrue, and tell yourself the affirmation anyway, there is a conflict. What you feel is another way that your subconscious perceives your belief or what you hold as true. It is important that your feelings are in alignment with your affirmations and your desires, beliefs, and expectations. Remember, emotions (feelings) are energy. You may be asking, "But what if I don't believe what I am telling myself?" Do it anyway. It is better than focusing the energy of your emotions, desires, and beliefs in a negative direction. It is also a step in the direction you want to proceed.

The Law of Dominant Effect

There is an important law about hypnosis called the Law of Dominant Effect. It tells us that whatever dominates our thought, whatever dominates our belief, is what our bodies are going to act upon. So if 51 percent of your mind believes "A" and only 49 percent of your mind believes "B," you are going to get "A," what the majority, or the dominance, of your thoughts is. This means that you don't have to have absolutely perfect belief; you just have to have the dominance of your belief focused on what you want. Certainly, this is a case where "more is better."

A Gastric Bypass Worked Magic

Margie struggled with her weight for many years. Thirty pounds were making her miserable. One day she watched a daytime talk show that changed her life. The guests on the show spoke of having had a new type of surgery called gastric bypass in which their intestines were bypassed so that only a portion of the foods they ate could be absorbed. They were enthusiastic while describing what sounded like effortless weight loss without dieting or exercise. One comment that really struck Margie in particular was, "The food just went right through me and was unabsorbed." This was in April.

In June, Margie's husband, Howard, looked at her and casually asked, "Have you lost weight?" She got up abruptly and left the room without saying a word. He dismissed her reaction, thinking that she was being overly sensitive about her weight. A few days later, noticing that she was radiantly happy and she did look thinner, he asked again, "Are you losing weight?"

She again left the room abruptly without a word. Howard wondered if something was wrong. While noticing that she seemed happier, he also noted that she was preparing sumptuous meals and luscious deserts that were usually taboo. This scene replayed until a week later when he followed her to the bedroom and told her that she looked thinner and he wanted to know if she was all right, or if some health problem was causing her weight loss. She said, "I don't want to talk about it." He persisted and she admitted, "Nothing is wrong, I am just afraid that if I talk about it the spell will be broken."

Margie told him about seeing people on TV who had gastric bypass surgery. They lost weight, did not diet, and could eat what they liked because the food went right through them. She said that when she lay in bed that night, she told herself that she had gastric bypass surgery and now the food went right through her. She then pretended what it might be like to lose weight this way. A few days later she was troubled by diarrhea and frequent urgent trips to the bathroom. She called the physician's office to make an appointment, and the nurse asked her to describe her problems. She told the nurse about the diarrhea and heard herself saying, "The food goes right through me—it's as if I've had a ..." and hung up the phone thinking, "Oh my God! It's working!" She realized that almost immediately after a meal or snack, she had to go to the bathroom. She felt just like the guests on the TV show.

Margie's energy was up and her spirits were even higher. By the end of the month, she had lost eighteen pounds. She was eating whatever she desired. To Margie, it seemed to be magic, and she feared that speaking with others might undermine her belief and change its power. Howard observed that she had lost weight and was eating without restraint, but he also noticed changes that she was unaware of. She was no longer snacking, her food choices were much wiser, her portion sizes were smaller, and she had much more energy and was more active. She was eating better because she felt better.

As the years passed, whenever her weight needed adjustment, she would give herself an imaginary gastric bypass until she regained her perfect weight. You certainly don't have to give yourself a gastric bypass, but this story vividly illustrates the power of belief. Just imagine what beliefs you can make true for *you*.

Time Is on Your Side

You do not have to be concerned about how long any patterns or programs have been running in your subconscious or mind-body. They can change the instant you discover what needs to be corrected or realigned, as well as when you make the deliberate choice to change them. We would like you to know how your mind-body understands time. You are aware of the linear and mechanical measurement of time in days, hours, minutes, and seconds—what we call "clock time." That is the way your conscious mind understands the measurement of time. Your subconscious, your mind-body, only understands "now time," where one minute can seem like ten, or ten minutes can seem like one, or everything is happening in the "now." In your sleep, you can experience a dream occurring in the place you lived as a child, but with people who went to your high school, people you will see at tomorrow's scheduled meeting, and the person who took your order for lunch that day. All this can occur at the same time in your dream because your subconscious perceives all time as "now." During your trancework you will hear Dr. G. mention that your subconscious can use the hypnotic suggestions along with images and ideas of the future as if they have already occurred. Since all time is "now time" to your subconscious, you can adjust, replace, or create the ideas and programs that you want to "run" within you right "now."

Changed Forever

Roger Bannister, a British athlete, is a great example of an individual who chose to believe in himself. Until 1954, when he broke the record time for running the mile in less than four minutes, the world believed that it could not be done. Yet within one year of his achievement, thirty-seven other runners around the world also ran the mile in under four minutes. When your beliefs about something change, they do not revert to old beliefs that no longer hold true. As you make changes, adjustments, and realignments in your beliefs, they are forever changed. New beliefs are contagious and spread rapidly.

Check in with yourself. Tell yourself that your past experience with dieting and weight loss is not a predictor of your success. Your success is predicted by your motivation, beliefs, and expectations. You will see what you believe.

BELIEF BOOSTER

Reality is what we take to be true.

What we take to be true is what we believe.

What we believe is based upon our perceptions.

What we perceive depends upon what we look for.

What we look for depends upon what we think.

What we think depends upon what we perceive.

What we perceive determines what we believe.

What we believe determines what we take to be true.

What we take to be true is our reality.

GARY ZUKAV

Is It All in Your Mind?

At this point, you may be wondering if the ideas you are reading about beliefs and self-hypnosis are "all in your mind." That is a fair question. It was commonly thought that hypnosis was a psychological experience that only involved the mind. However, research shows that it involves both the body and mind. A study reported in the *American Journal of Psychiatry* (2000) used PET brain scans to observe the areas of the brain activated by color and gray shades. They found that when hypnotized subjects were shown the gray shade but were told it was color, the parts of the brain that process color were activated and the gray-shade processing areas were not. And when they were shown the color pattern but were told it was a gray shade, only the areas of the brain that process gray shades were activated.

A study in *NeuroImage* (2004) used functional MRI brain scanning to observe the parts of the brain activated by pain. Subjects were given hypnotic suggestions to experience pain. The researchers found that hypnotically induced pain and physically produced pain activated the very same parts of the brain.

What these studies tell us is, "Yes, it is in your mind ... and your body." Your body responds to beliefs, ideas, expectations, and hypnotic suggestions as real in a very physical way.

How do you want your body to respond?

Earlier in this chapter we said that your past experience with dieting and weight loss is not a predictor of your future success. If at any time you notice that what is happening is not what you want to happen, you can change it. Let us say that you discover that the road you are on is not taking you where you want to go. You do not have to backtrack through every single turn that got you this far. You can simply change the course. The talented guitarist and teacher Jamie Andreas tells her students, "There are no 'mistakes,' only unwanted results." We really like this concept. Even what you might think of as a mistake is not a mistake at all. It is the direct result of what you have been doing, and the way you have been doing it. Remember, you cannot make any mistakes with the Self-Hypnosis Diet. You can make no mistakes in your achievement of weight loss. If any unwanted results occur, you simply change or adjust some things. You might adjust how you are wanting or believing, or what you expect, or you might change your feelings. If you don't like the results, change what you are doing. You can change what is creating the results until the results are consistent with what you want to have happen. Whenever you notice unwanted results, you can map out a new course for where you want to go. Your new map includes what you want, believe, and expect, with a feeling of gratitude and trust that it is guaranteed.

Do not waste your time or energy even thinking about what you do *not* want. Even worse than that is wasting your energy on what you might think of as obstacles or resistance to your achievement. Merely thinking in these directions gives energy to them. Focus your thought and belief energy only on the results you want to enjoy. Thoughts, beliefs, and expectations are energy. Use your energy wisely. All energy should be directed to your positive results.

IN THEIR OWN WORDS ...

I have been using self-hypnosis for two weeks and have noticed a dramatic reduction in my sugar cravings, which were completely out of hand before! I also noticed that I'm not experiencing "the blues" like I usually do when I try to cut back on or eliminate sweets. And, my weight is finally dropping!

TONY

Belief Never Fails ... Even When False

Belief does not fail, ever. Your beliefs and expectations will never fail you. They will always prove themselves true, even when they are false beliefs. In 2005, Dr. Elizabeth Loftus presented the results of a study on false beliefs to the National Academy of Science. She suggested a false belief (something untrue) that a certain food once made the study subjects ill when they were children. The results showed that the individuals later avoided eating that food, which was acting out the belief *as true*. Are you acting out something *as true*? Examine if it is a belief that benefits you.

We love remembering what Henry Ford said: "If you believe you can or believe you can't, you're right."

CHAPTER 3

SIMPLY PRACTICING HYPNOSIS

Whatever you can do, or dream you can, begin it.
Boldness has genius, power, and magic in it.

GOETHE

We all simply want time to relax, to dream, to pretend. It is refreshing to the physical body and rejuvenating to the spirit. When we practice our hypnosis, it offers us just that: a very personal time to enliven and enrich our mind and body. The practice is done simply. You need nothing more than a comfortable and safe place.

A Few Simple Rules

There are some rules to hypnosis, and they ensure that your practice is the most efficient and yields the greatest benefits. When you are ready to begin using the CDs, find a comfortable and safe place in your home or office where you can sit in a chair, recline, or even lie down. Make sure you are relaxed and in a place where you do not have to pay attention to anything else. Do not listen to your trancework while you are driving a car or operating any type of machinery. It is helpful to decide on a regular time each day or night to practice your self-hypnosis. Bedtime is a good opportunity to enjoy your trancework, and practicing at this time can be a wonderful way to enter a restful sleep.

> ## IN THEIR OWN WORDS ...
> The trancework has truly assisted me in engaging the unconscious to support my conscious goals. I'm ready to start in twice a day. Just listening through twice has already influenced my food choices this past week.
> MARK

Distractions and interruptions are inevitable. Rather than allow them to annoy you and take you away from your trancework, use them. Use the sounds in the environment around you to enhance your trance experience. For example, while doing your hypnosis you may notice a sound and start thinking that this sound is distracting you. You then become more focused on this distraction than on your hypnosis. You may be tempted to struggle against it—which takes energy away from the hypnosis. Instead, when you notice a sound that at first seems distracting or annoying, take control of it by giving it your *permission* to be there as a background sound. Give it an assignment, such as thinking to yourself that "the sound of the barking dog is helping me go deeper and deeper within" or "the fan motor sounds like a waterfall that is a soothing background sound." At our private practice in Tucson, there is a day school that inevitably lets the children out to play during one of our hypnosis sessions. That is when we suggest, "The sound of children can be a background sound that lets you go deeper and deeper within yourself now." This is part of our "use everything" philosophy.

Distractions also include the sensations you might experience within you. For example, you may find yourself noticing

THE SELF-HYPNOSIS DIET

a part of your body that itches. The more you focus on the itching or on scratching the itch, the less you are focusing your consciousness on the trance. At those times, you simply remind yourself that you have permission to move your attention back to your trance or daydream and let the itch go unscratched. When working with patients who have pain disorders, we teach them to focus attention away from the "distraction" of pain in a similar way. After all, we cannot control the environment around us or the sensations within us, but we can choose where we focus our attention. If you have trouble letting go of an annoying distraction, you may have to command that it be there as a background sound or sensation, which then lets you go more comfortably within. Detach yourself from anything that is competing with your attention to your hypnosis. Let go of any struggle with the environment. Just let it be there, and sooner or later you will no longer notice it. When you learn to accept a sensation, noise, or other element that interferes with your hypnosis, you no longer allow it to have control over you.

Law of Reversed Effect

There is a law in hypnosis, called the Law of Reversed Effect, that says that sometimes the more you try to do something, the more it does not happen. An example is when you want to say a name that you know you know—it may be a book title, a person, a movie—but you cannot say it at that moment, and the more you try, the less it is there. The name comes when you suggest to your subconscious mind that "I'll remember later" or "It'll come to me later." By letting go of the question "What's the name? What's the name?" you have released your subconscious mind to now retrieve and deliver the answer, and it always does. So, the Law of Reversed Effect is that when you are trying too hard for something, it only gives you the opposite (the reverse).

Simple Techniques

SUBCONSCIOUS
MIND
(OR UNCONSCIOUS
MIND)
This is the portion
of our psyche that
performs functions
and processes
below our thinking
awareness. It is
the mind of the
body. It breathes
us, digests, pulses
our hearts, and in
general, manages
our involuntary
physical processes
for us. It can also
tell us to choose
a piece of fresh
mango instead of
chocolate cake, to
stop eating when
we are full, or to
enjoy a walk in
the park.

Becoming absorbed in your thoughts and ideas is that gentle journey into the center of yourself called "going into trance." The simple techniques of self-hypnosis include going into trance, deepening the trance, using that trance-state to give messages and suggestions to the mind-body, and coming out of trance.

Going Into Trance

When you are using the trancework on the CD, I will be your guide as you go into trance. I will use a trance induction method that you will find calming and focusing. You have probably seen the swinging watch method in movies, which in thirty-five years of practice I have never seen anyone use; but there are many different ways to focus your attention to go into trance. You might stare at a spot on the wall, use a breathing technique, or use progressive body relaxation. You will hear a variety of induction methods on the trancework CD. They are merely the cues or the signals that you are giving to yourself to say "I am going into trance" or "I am going to do my hypnosis now." Going into trance can also be thought of as "letting yourself daydream … deliberately." You are letting yourself become absorbed in your thoughts and ideas, very absorbed, and allowing yourself to pretend or imagine what you desire as achieved and real. There is no "going under." Instead, there is a lovely experience of going within.

Deepening the Trance

Deepening your trance helps you become more absorbed in your thoughts, ideas, and experience. This is done with progressive relaxation: going "deeper and deeper within …" with images or scenes, or by counting a number sequence, for example. We like to suggest that as you hear the counting from ten down to zero, you create a vertical imagery that is associated with going deeper, such as a path leading down a mountain or into a lush green valley. As you hear me counting, you can picture or imagine going more deeply into a scene or place that is even more enjoyable and comfortable to you. This is what we mean by "deepening the trance."

Talking to the Mind of Your Body with Messages and Suggestions

During the trancework, you will hear my voice speaking to two parts of your mind. One part of your mind is your conscious thinking mind. That is the part of you that is excellent at telling time, making change, learning how to read and write; it is your "thinking mind." Throughout the trancework, your thinking mind will continue doing its normal activity of having thoughts. So you don't have to worry about clearing your mind, or emptying your mind, or putting your mind totally at peace. Simply notice that your mind will continue "thinking," and your job is to unplug or disconnect just enough so that you do not have to react to those thoughts. You give them permission to stream by. If your "to do" list keeps popping up, for example, just allow it to stream by, rather than dwell on it.

The other part of your mind I will be speaking to is what we call your subconscious mind—"sub" because it is below your thinking level of awareness. It is the "mind of your body." Your subconscious mind has the wisdom to manage your body's trillions of cells, your body chemistry, and all the body's functions of breathing, digestion, the nervous system, the endocrine system, and the immune system. The mind-body has an immense amount of wisdom, and, in doing your hypnosis, you are accumulating and acquiring additional wisdom that the mind of your body will act upon, consistent with

CONSCIOUS MIND This is the "thinking mind" or the part of the psyche that gives us our awareness or sense of knowing and governs our voluntary functions. For example, our conscious mind takes that second piece of pie at the buffet, swipes the debit card at the grocery store, and moves the fork to our mouth.

your motivation, your beliefs, and your expectations, to help you with your weight loss.

You always have the opportunity to adjust and tailor the words being spoken or the images described to best fit you. This tailoring process is very important. It has to fit *you* because it is *your* self-hypnosis and all hypnosis is self-hypnosis. As we've said, hypnosis is not something done to you. It is something that you are being guided to experience, and as you experience it, you are learning it. Repetition and rehearsal create solid ability and knowledge within you. You might even call it subconscious knowledge because your subconscious mind can carry it out for you without your having to even think of it. So the thoughts and ideas that may have been troubling you about your weight, or your inability to lose weight, are now being changed to something that supports your perfect body. And your mind-body is memorizing the experience so that it can refer to that experience instead of the unwanted results of the past.

For example, if you believe that you are a "yo-yo" dieter because you have always regained the weight you have lost, you may use your trancework to suggest, "Every day I am losing weight and my body remembers how to make this a permanent ability. I am achieving my perfect weight." Subconscious knowledge, or the mind-body wisdom that is learned from your trancework, is very much like when you learned to ride a bicycle or drive a car. When you were first learning, there seemed to be many things to pay attention to at the same time, but very quickly your mind-body took on this knowledge so that now you can drive safely and you do not even have to tell your feet what to do.

One of our clients, Amy, told us that when she first began using self-hypnosis, she would tell her body what she wanted her ideal weight to be. She would carefully and vividly dial in the set-point of body weight with an image of adjusting a thermostat to the number of pounds she desired. She focused her attention on these images. Her mind-body responded with some creative outcomes. She discovered that her weight fluctuated within only a plus- or minus-five-pound range around the set-point she imagined. As if automatically, when her weight increased, she would experience a craving for fruits and vegetables and would forget about desserts. She also felt more inclined to exercise and would feel full before completing a meal. She described the results: "It is as if my body has an autopilot to make these adjustments automatically for me now."

Coming Out of Trance

At the end of the trancework sessions, you will hear me speaking about letting your body awaken with a feeling of refreshment and well-being, and bringing that refreshment with you to the front surface of your mind, so that you come out of trance feeling comfortably renewed and alert. Or, when doing your hypnosis at bedtime, you may drift into a deep, restful sleep.

After you are alert, it is important to debrief. This is the time to make a note or two for yourself if thoughts or ideas came to mind that would be useful to you. Often during trance, not only are you giving messages to your body, but your body is talking to *you,* and you will be listening to the mind of your body. Your body may share very useful information and you may want to write it down.

For instance, let us say you have a particular food that you just cannot resist, a food like French fries that has been your "downfall" in dieting. During the trancework, you may get an insight (something you heard when you listened to the mind of your body) that tells you why French fries became an obstacle or even a "comfort" to you emotionally. That insight now allows you to choose what you want and not just carry out the previous pattern that was established, perhaps decades ago, and born out of some emotional experience that is now long past and no longer valid in your life.

. Jennifer was diligent and hard working in every area of her life and almost every aspect of her weight loss program. She exercised every day, ate lots of fruits and vegetables, drank plenty of water, enjoyed grains, and even bought organically when she was able. She made very wise choices for health, but remained twenty pounds over her perfect weight. As she sat miserably in our office, she told of her seemingly insatiable desire for ice cream (organic though it was) every night and every social opportunity that presented itself. During her trancework we asked if there was a part of her that knew why she seemed to crave ice cream. She was silent for several minutes, and then reiterated the long-ago words of her loving grandfather: "Jenny, dear, ice cream is the best reward for hard work, so eat up while it lasts, it may be gone tomorrow, just like me." Once she uncovered the source of her ice cream craving, she was able to enjoy it but not eat it so often.

The Time Has Come ...

The time has come for you to simply listen and savor your first taste of self-hypnosis. The CD inside the back cover of the book contains the tracks of trancework. You will begin your experience with self-hypnosis by listening to tracks 1 and 2. Track 1 is a brief introduction and instructional audio regarding the rules of practicing self-hypnosis. Track 2 is an introduction to self-hypnosis, the "mind hors d'oeuvre" of the Self-Hypnosis Diet. You may enjoy this small sample on track 2 as many times as you wish.

So simply listen and savor. As you listen, I would like you to think of me as if I were in the same room with you. Imagine me as your personal guide. When you close your eyes, I am right there with you. Let my voice go with you as you practice your self-hypnosis. This is just for you. Now is the perfect time for your first taste of the Self-Hypnosis Diet.

... What Was the Experience Like for You?

Now that you have had experience with self-hypnosis, what did you experience? Were you "hypnotized"? Did you go into a hypnotic trance? The majority of individuals who are new to hypnosis will question whether or not they actually experienced it. You may feel the same way. If you were expecting a profoundly altered state of consciousness, then you have discovered that there really is no "going under" and no loss of consciousness. In fact, you were aware of where you were and what you were doing most, if not all, of the time. We hear a variation on the same theme when people have completed their first experience with self-hypnosis: "That was amazing (or incredible, or extraordinary, or remarkable)."

When I am asked what *I* experience when in trance, an example from my college years comes to mind: I was staring out the window during a lecture. I knew the professor was lecturing, I could hear his voice, but I did not have any idea what he was saying during those moments. Being in trance is very much like being in a daydream state. The major distinction between a trance and a daydream is that the trance is a very deliberate type of daydream wherein you are absorbed in ideas that you want your mind-body to share. When in trance, you have an intention to provide your mind-body with ideas or suggestions about what you want it to do for you.

We are always delighted to hear people say after their first trance experience, "I liked it. I did not want it to end." Then we *know* that they experienced trance and discovered that they *can* do it.

Hypnotic Phenomena

Trance is a very subtle experience. You can review the subtleties of what you felt, what you noticed *not noticing,* and what you experienced. Some people may feel heavy, their arms and legs seemingly immovable; or they may feel light, weightless, or floating. Some will feel warm or cool, or become so absorbed in the mental imagery that they feel as if they are actually there, present in their imagery. Parts of the body may seem to disappear so completely that they are not even noticed. It is also normal to experience time differently. One minute may seem like ten minutes or ten minutes may seem like only one. These are normal experiences we call "hypnotic phenomena." If you are familiar with daydreaming, you already know that most of what is called hypnotic phenomena is also normal waking-state phenomena as well. How many times have you "awakened" from a daydream, or been roused from an interesting book or movie to find that a suprising amount of time has elapsed?

The possible range of phenomena with hypnosis is extensive, including hypnoanalgesia (the reduction of pain) and hypnoanesthesia (the elimination of pain). When in trance, an individual can actually imagine that a part or all of her body is so comfortably numb that she can undergo a surgical procedure using hypnosis as the sole anesthetic.

You will be happy to know that hypnotic phenomena can be produced that are particularly useful for weight loss. You may be able to create, for example, a physical sensation of fullness, or a craving for nourishing food. You may be able to create a sensation of enhanced taste or smell. You may even be able to forget about foods that are not consistent with your weight loss goals. You may even be surprised to feel a craving for exercise.

Remember the power of self-hypnosis. You can choose what you want to say to your mind-body. You can choose what you want your mind-body to do for you. It is your choice, your perfect weight.

CHAPTER 4

PERFECT MIND— PERFECT WEIGHT

Sometimes I've believed as many as six
impossible things before breakfast.
LEWIS CARROLL, *Alice's Adventures in Wonderland*

Perfect mind and perfect weight." The phrase may sound like a myth to you. What are perfect mind and perfect weight? They are the realistic terms you can use as you pursue weight loss. "Realistic?" you ask. "How can anything be 'perfect,' let alone my weight and my thoughts about my weight?" Well, remember what we said about the power of belief and believing. Would it serve your interest to ever desire or aspire to anything less than perfection for yourself? Indulge us here for a while as we explain why you can think of your mind and weight as "perfect."

Perfect weight is the weight that is right for *you*. It is the weight that is achievable and consistent with what you want and what you are willing to give yourself and accept for yourself. More importantly, your perfect weight gives you the body that is healthy, the body that moves with ease, and the one in which you feel good about yourself and happy. And what is perfect mind? You already have a perfect mind.

It is flawless. However, there may be some thoughts in that perfect mind of yours that are giving you unwanted results. There may be something you hold in mind, perhaps habits or patterns, which give you unwanted results. But you can use your perfect mind to align your thoughts to give you what you want. You can use your mind to achieve the body weight you want.

> Perfect weight is not about perfectionism. Perfect weight is about trusting your body, your food, and the lifestyle you have created to naturally maintain your healthiest and happiest weight.

In the Twinkling of an Eye

Your present body is the result of your thoughts and beliefs. You have acted out these thoughts and beliefs through your lifestyle, which created your present weight. You have not made any mistakes, despite what you might be thinking of yourself; rather, you have just experienced unwanted results. These unwanted results are a direct consequence of misaligned thoughts and beliefs about yourself that have become patterns of behavior or lifestyle. *The Self-Hypnosis Diet* is about using your perfect mind to align your thoughts to give you the results you want. You really *can* use your mind to achieve the body weight you want.

Let us look at some of the learning that has taken place in your life that has gotten you to where you are now with your body weight. Did you wake up one morning, and there you were with the extra pounds? Or was it a gradual accumulation over time? Or maybe you have known nothing else since early childhood. Whatever the case, there are many factors that created your present body:

- food choices
- eating habits
- the self-critic in you
- economic background
- emotional background
- influence of family
- influence of friends
- cultural background

These and many other factors were *learned* in your life and became your beliefs, which in turn became patterns of action that produced your present body.

We will be more specific. Notice which of the following factors seem true for you in your earlier years. That is, think about what you *did* learn in your childhood about food and eating.

- What types of groceries did your family purchase?
- What foods did your parents cook, and how were they usually prepared?
- Did you eat exclusively at home or frequently grab fast food?
- Were you served fresh, wholesome, home-cooked foods, or did you eat mostly processed and highly refined foods, fried foods, and "junk" food?
- Was there mindful attention to nutrition, or was there reckless disregard for what your family ate?
- What did you learn about eating mindfully?
- Were you taught that healthy food choices led to healthier bodies?
- Did anyone teach you how to know what is healthy food and what is not?
- Were your food choices based on what tasted or looked good or cost less?

• Did your family or school teach you about healthy lifestyles and sound nutrition, or was your "nutrition education" via TV commercials and food manufacturers' advertisements?

What *did* you learn as a child? What became your beliefs about eating, food, and your body? Examine your socio-economic or socio-cultural origins, and see if they had an influence on how and what you learned to eat. Over thirty-five years ago, sociological studies pointed out weight problems in the lower and working class based on their consumption patterns of what has been referred to as "poverty-level foods," such as hot dogs, canned meats, and processed luncheon meats. Cultural groups have also been studied to understand how their dietary patterns and foods, such as cooking with lard or eating a diet of high-fat and fried foods, may result in greater body fat. These influences are easily accepted since they are "normal" to the group or class.

Next, let us look at your adolescent years. During adolescence, were there any changes in your weight? As a boy, were you encouraged to heap more food on your plate? "Look at him eat! Surely he is going to grow into a big man!" (There is a telling metaphor!) Or were you admonished to eat less? When you were a budding young girl, did a wise woman take you under her wing and share with you the marvel of menses and the wonderment of body changes, including the natural increase in body fat with the development of breasts and wider hips? Were you aware during puberty that unless your body naturally increased body fat by at least 22 percent, it would not properly mature and produce menses? Or was all that "hushed up" as an embarrassing development? It was probably during adolescence that you learned there is a stigma regarding overweight people. Spend a few minutes writing down the factors that seem to be true for you in your earlier years. Ponder the experiences and influences that are still shaping your present body.

In high school, the athletes in school sports were always a healthy weight, and so were the cheerleaders and homecoming queens. What early beliefs about your popularity and self-image may have formed from your social interactions in high school? What did you learn about physical activity and what habits did you create? Were you introduced to physical activity as part of a healthy lifestyle, through sports or family outings of hikes or walks? Or was the blaring TV a standard fixture, enticing everyone to the couch?

Next is a question that most people have not been mindful of during their development. As you were growing up, was the focus of self-care centered on fashionable clothing, makeup, and hairstyles, or on wholesome food, regular physical activity, and intellectual and spiritual nourishment? What about now? Spend a few more minutes writing down the factors that seem to be true for you in recent years. What experiences and influences formed the thoughts, which turned into the beliefs, which turned into your present body?

BELIEF BOOSTER

Obesity increases risk of developing hypertension, diabetes, and metabolic syndrome, which increase risk for heart attacks and strokes. Metabolic syndrome refers to a number of conditions, including abdominal obesity, high triglycerides, high LDL (bad) cholesterol, high blood pressure, and high levels of blood sugar.

After high school, you probably moved away from home. Suddenly you were no longer captive to your family's lifestyle. Did you become more mindful of your choices, or did you begin eating with disregard? If you entered into a close relationship, what compromises or agreements regarding food and physical activity did you enter into also? Most relationships develop out of similar interests, such as food preferences and eating styles. Ultimately, the relationship includes eating patterns and preferences that are a result of compromise. Have your relationships encouraged wise food choices and healthy eating? Perhaps you have experienced pregnancy. Did you learn how to have a healthy pregnancy and nourish a healthy baby within you? Or did you add pounds onto pounds? After giving birth, did your lifestyle help you regain your normal weight or inhibit it? If you were active in sports or league games, did your career or family responsibilities take priority and remove these fitness activities from your routine? Did you adjust diet and exercise accordingly, or did the weight start to accumulate? Did an injury, accident, or illness occur that disrupted a regular physical activity that was supportive of healthy weight?

IN THEIR OWN WORDS ...

For me, being one of the people about whom doctors write "morbid obesity" in their charts, it seems the more I saturate my unconscious with this wisdom, the better. I now find myself *not* giving myself nutritional advice from the "outside in" as it were, but from deep within as it "wells up." The gentle suggestions don't always come up from within in the form of words, but I find myself actually making decisions based on these … feelings— and so far the decisions I've made have been for my great nutritional benefit.

JANE

As you can see, how you got to where you are *now* was certainly no accident. You learned from the people around you—or you absorbed from your environment—how to make food choices, how to eat, how to take care of yourself physically and emotionally. Whether the ideas you learned were good and healthful or not so good and not so healthful, they became your beliefs, and became you and your body as it is today. Remember, you did not do anything wrong, but you have experienced the results of living and eating that were consistent with your thoughts and beliefs.

MOTIVATION MAKER

The September 2005 issue of *First for Women* included a story and photos of a woman who went from a weight of 280 pounds down to 148 pounds. She described seeing her five-year-old son glued to the window, watching their neighbor family play a game of soccer. She thought, *I know he wants to play more than anything, but we'd better stay inside. That kind of activity could kill me.* She made the decision right then and there to change. She listed the changes she made in behavior, eating, and exercise, remarking that "my motivation coach (her son) was there 24/7." Her desire to join her son became an amazing motivation catalyst. In the twinkling of an eye, you can put the energy of your desire and beliefs into action, and you are inspiring yourself to do it.

Chapter 6 is devoted to exploring emotional factors in greater detail, but we have just one more question for you at this point. Over the years, what has been your response to people and their comments about your weight, good or bad? Did you go out and buy a good pair of running shoes, or did you eat to ease the emotional discomfort? Perhaps you even learned the latter reaction in your childhood. Did your mother ever give you a plateful of food to comfort you when you were unhappy? These are all learned responses, and they can be unlearned and replaced with new responses and patterns to create your perfect weight. You ask, "How long will this take?" We tell you, "In the twinkling of an eye." For the moment you realize that you want it enough to do anything to have it, it is done. You have just changed the direction of a powerful energy within you that will now be directed toward learning how to achieve the results that you want: your perfect weight.

> **MOTIVATION MAKER**
>
> Take a few minutes to write in a journal a description of your strong and energetic body, and what activities it performs so well for you.

Your Perfect Mind Relearning

It is easy to understand how you acquired or "learned" to weigh more than your perfect weight. And it will be easy to make new choices, to relearn new patterns, and to create new and more healthful habits. How do we learn? We learn by modeling another person, studying books (like this one), using other resources (listed in the appendix of this book), and practicing the actions that produce the results we seek. The most effective and lasting learning involves practice and repetition. How you practice is supremely important.

Pretend for a moment that you are a violinist. You are rehearsing for a grand symphony performance in New York City. Your piece has a segment of five bars that are very difficult for your fingers to play correctly. There are two ways for you to practice. The first, which is very ineffective, is to play that difficult segment quickly, over and over and over again, continually playing the same mistakes, but hoping your fingers will finally play it correctly. The second way to practice, which is always successful, is to play the segment very, very slowly, mindfully "teaching" your fingers how to move, creating the "muscle memory" for the correct movements, until your fingers have learned the movements and can play the entire segment correctly and at the proper tempo with little, if any, conscious attention.

The important point here is that you are giving your attention to *practicing correctly.* By being mindful of what you are practicing, and how you are practicing it, you are learning the new patterns that are replacing the old patterns. You are practicing the activity that produces your perfect body weight.

You, too, can create "muscle memory" by practicing mindful eating (eating slowly, chewing thoroughly, swallowing the last bite before you take the next bite) or a more mindful, slower fork-to-mouth movement. You can also practice an entire dining style that becomes conditioned as a mind-body memory or learning, which quickly becomes automatic. As it becomes automatic or second nature, you do not have to even think about it.

MUSCLE MEMORY
Practice occurs when we repeat a particular sequence of physical movements until the muscles have "memorized" the movements and mind awareness is no longer necessary. Examples: typing on a keyboard, riding a bicycle, knitting.

Practice the Results You Want

Let's put some thought into determining your perfect weight. After all, you need to practice the "perfect" you before it can become real for you. First, however, we must debunk several false "ideal images" in our culture. Think for a moment about what comes to mind when you consider the "ideal body." The svelte athlete and the tall willowy model are the false "ideal images" plastered on every glossy magazine cover and portrayed in every TV advertisement and Hollywood movie. We are talking about weight in this book, so we won't even mention the perfect hair, perfect teeth and smile, perfect nose, flawless complexion, and perfectly sculpted body. Right now, we're just focusing on weight. In reality, these "ideal images" are slyly crafted composites, created through the lens of a camera, with layers of make-up, and crews on the sidelines with brushes, sprays, glitter, and other photographic magic. Underneath it all is often a young person, sadly emaciated, with a modeling career centered on food deprivation and skin-deep beauty. Not very pleasant, is it? Not very real either, is it?

So throw away the "ideal images" of our culture, and begin your practice. Just pretend how your perfect weight will support you in every way. Dream about how healthy you will feel, how strong and energetic you will be, and how easily your body will move. Make believe how good you will feel about yourself, your renewed self-confidence and self-esteem. Visualize how much more you will enjoy your life, your friends, and your family. Envision it all. Think about your perfect weight and how it supports you in every way. Indulge in your fantasy, just as you did as a playful child. Indulge in your pretending, knowing that those reveries are just the beginning of creating the new patterns that lead to your perfect weight. In other words, start living as if you have already achieved the results you want.

> **MOTIVATION MAKER**
>
> A Harvard School of Public Health study published recently in the *Journal of the American Medical Association* revealed that for every two hours spent watching television daily, obesity spiraled by 23 percent and type 2 diabetes by 14 percent. Both lack of physical activity and snacking while viewing played central roles in these statistics.

Start Where You Are Today

A Chinese proverb says: "A journey of a thousand miles begins with a single step." You simply start where you are at this moment, taking your steps toward your perfect weight. Yesterday and tomorrow are not now. Start where you are today. You begin by discovering and experimenting with new patterns, new behaviors, and new choices that influence your perfect weight.

These new thoughts begin to crowd out those old patterns that gave you unwanted results. It is much like going on a clothes shopping spree. When you hang new clothes in your closet, you make room by folding up the old clothes and putting them in a bag for someone else. Making positive choices based on what you want and putting them in mind, along with doing your self-hypnosis, will help you comfortably adopt all the new patterns, behaviors, and choices that influence your perfect weight. Let go of all hope for a better past, and proceed with what you can do right now. As you go forward making changes each day, you are accumulating a recent past that supports giving you the perfect weight you have chosen.

MOTIVATION MAKER

Keep a Beginner's Mind

When beginning to learn any new skill, you approach it with an open and fresh mind, giving it much attention. There is a Zen teaching that says the first time you do something, you put your attention on what you are doing. You give it your full attention. But the second time you do it, you are not as fully present, which may make you become numb to the experience. Keep the beginner's mind fresh in you, remain eager to learn more, and remain mindful of what you are doing and practicing. Each step you make takes you toward the results that you want. This is also a wonderful way to enhance the pleasure of each bite of a meal. You make each bite the "first" bite, which is so very full of flavor and satisfaction, rather than ignore what you are eating and focus on the next bite.

PARAPHRASED FROM JAMIE ANDREAS,
The Principles of Correct Practice for Guitar

Everything Is a Choice

Everything is a choice. If you consciously agree to what you read here and what you hear during the trancework, your subconscious says, "Yes!" or "I'll do it for you!" That is, your subconscious mind, your mind-body, will reflect what you choose and agree to accept or believe. Just as you can choose what to believe, you can choose what to learn. And with repetition and consistency, you are creating the learned responses that quickly become automatic or second nature. So, in essence, the choices you are making, along with the thoughts and actions you correctly practice, give you the results you desire.

Approach Your Goal Like a Hobby

> ## MOTIVATION MAKER
>
> WOW! Sixty-five percent of Americans are overweight. Start compiling interesting tidbits of information about food and fitness that many people are not even aware of. You can search the Internet or subscribe to a health magazine or e-newsletter. Treat weight loss as your "hobby," and you will absorb lots of these tidbits. Here is one to start the list: It takes thirty-five minutes of brisk walking to work off the calories in one soda. Drink water.

INTENTION AND ATTENTION
Intention is the mental idea of what you want. Attention is the energy placed on what you are doing that will give you the results that you want. Make your intention clear and fuel it with your desire. Then give your actions the attention needed to bring about the results you intend.

Hobbies give us the satisfaction of learning new things and occupying our minds with pleasant experiences that lead to an outcome that also pleases us. Approach your weight loss effort as if it were a new hobby. Indulge yourself in magazines, tools, and books, perhaps even classes and interest groups. Dedicate a special area of your home to your hobby. Just as other hobbies give you a refreshing break from work activities, let your weight loss hobby also serve to give you a refreshing alternative to your job or work. Even when you are at work, you may find wonderful ways to incorporate time and attention to this hobby. In this regard, begin to explore all of the resources available to your new recreational interest, i.e., your weight loss hobby. Be on the lookout for anything that serves your hobby interests. The Internet, bookstores, libraries, and newsstands are full of resources for you. You do not know where some of the simplest, yet most powerfully inspiring ideas will come to you. Do not limit yourself to diets and advertisements about weight loss. Let everything in this world now serve your hobby. You are creating this hobby. Enjoy it for yourself exclusively.

Magnificent Makeover

Now this is a very special idea for you to make your weight loss both enjoyable and effortless. You may be like many others who have found dieting and exercise to be monumental chores, smacking of obligation. It does not have to be that way. We propose that you approach your weight loss as if it were a very special prize or reward. Many television shows have selected individuals for a "makeover" where they may get the royal treatment in changing their appearance in some positive way. They usually do rapid makeovers with makeup, hair styles, and clothing. Allow yourself the luxury of accepting a magnificent makeover of your body weight. Put the idea in your mind that any weight loss activity is now part of your magnificent makeover. And this makeover is very special, for you are exploring, adopting, and integrating lifetime patterns of eating wholesome foods, enjoying healthy exercise, and keeping

your body in the shape and condition that make you proud, confident, and satisfied with yourself. Allow this magnificent makeover
to be a very special prize. So special that you embrace all the new
activities, new food choices, and powerful beliefs deeply in your
subconscious mind. The trancework we have prepared for you is
right on target for your magnificent makeover.

> ### MOTIVATION MAKER
> *First Steps in the Kitchen*
> Don't eat out as much. Learn a few basic cooking skills,
> like steaming and stir-frying. People eat *more* when
> they eat *out,* especially when they eat fast food.

You Can Ask for Anything

As we said at the beginning of this chapter, a perfect weight
may have sounded like a myth to you. But we are serious, and
we want you to be serious and committed to putting these
ideas into mind and practice. One of the nicest features about
self-hypnosis is that you can ask for and bring into subconscious
anything you desire. You deserve the weight that is perfect for
you, the weight that lets your body move freely with vitality and health, and the body that you are proud of creating
each day. Emotionally, these are the body and weight that lift
your spirits, build greater confidence, and free you from past
emotional and physical patterns that are no longer "perfect"
for you. In your mind, you are giving yourself a magnificent
makeover. Let yourself delight in all that contributes to your
perfect weight. This is your body, your life, and your business.
You are the only person you have to please. You are the only
person who can make you happy. By the *weigh,* what others
may think of your hobby, your methods, and your makeover,
is none of *your* business.

MOTIVATION MAKER

Lose Weight and Gain Wealth

A study in the *Economics and Human Biology* journal found that when very obese women decreased their body mass index by ten points, their net worth increased by $11,880. Surveys were conducted regarding home values, bank savings, and various other assets over a fifteen-year period. It is speculated that the obese may earn less than normal-weight individuals. In addition, there is a reduction in health-care costs after weight loss.

Ginny's "Absolutely Effortless" Hypnosis

Ginny had been on every diet and in every weight management program her small community offered. She knew just about everyone in her town, and she felt that everyone knew her as the overweight woman who was always on a diet or trying the latest weight loss fad. Whenever someone suggested a new program or diet, she cringed, anticipating yet another failure that everyone would know about. One day at the supermarket checkout, she saw a magazine that featured a secret method to lose weight but was not a diet. She bought it and read about a woman much like herself who had become very sensitized and sensitive about how others viewed her weight loss. The method she read about involved hypnosis. The article provided the name of a professional association of doctors who used hypnosis, and reading the article encouraged her to try just one visit to learn self-hypnosis. On her first visit, the doctor explained what hypnosis was and what it was not. After answering her questions, the doctor invited Ginny to experience a hypnotic trance. Although she was shaking on the inside, she agreed to proceed. As she reclined in a chair, the doctor spoke softly to her about hypnosis and relaxation. He presented several positive ideas about her ability to lose weight easily. For some reason, Ginny did not find herself fighting the ideas or analyzing them in either a negative or positive manner. The doctor described a lovely imaginary journey, and Ginny found herself so absorbed in the imagery that she noticed she was not paying conscious attention to the doctor. He just seemed to be a voice she heard, but she was not fully aware of what he was saying. In her imagination, she was absorbed with dancing at a wedding, wearing a size 12 dress that fit her perfectly. Many of the guests wanted to dance with her and paid her compliments. When he suggested that she return to a full waking state feeling refreshed, she followed the suggestion, but told him that she wanted to stay longer because it was so very pleasant. The doctor told her to practice this imaginative exercise each day for one month and then to return for a second visit.

When Ginny returned a month later, she had lost ten pounds and told the doctor how delighted she was with her hypnosis. She said that it seemed absolutely effortless. Yet, when the doctor asked what else had changed, she found herself describing many changes in eating patterns, different food choices, more energy, and more restful sleep with wonderful dreams in which she was at a happy weight. Further questioning by the doctor surprised her. She heard herself telling him that she was now going for daily walks, using the stairs instead of the elevator, no longer snacking or stopping for take-out meals, and she had even enrolled in dance lessons at the community college recreational center. She was not dieting, per se, but she was happily and comfortably involved in many activities that helped her achieve her weight loss. At an appointment later that year, she told the doctor that she never told anyone that she was creating her own version or method of weight loss, but she did tell people that she learned hypnosis. With tears of happiness, she also told the doctor that for the first time in her life, she was happy about what she found within her that created this change (nearly a forty-pound weight loss), and how proud she was of herself. And so was I.

BELIEF BOOSTER
One or two pounds per week is the
optimum weight loss goal.

CHAPTER 5

LOVE, LOVE ME DO

*You, yourself, as much as anybody in the entire
universe, deserve your love and affection.*
BUDDHA

Most people don't really think very much about self-love. We would like to help you indulge in this concept, and discover how much you really *can* love yourself. It is a prerequisite for creating and accepting your perfect weight—and everything else that is wonderful for you. Just being aware of the concept of self-love can move you further along on the path of loving yourself and accepting yourself as you are. Your nature and personality are reflections of how you feel about yourself. If you harbor resentment or guilt, or feel undeserving, these feelings work against loving yourself.

- How do you view your faults?
- Do you blame yourself? Self-love and finding fault or blaming yourself oppose each other. It's hard to fully love yourself when you often find fault.
- Do you place attention on negative aspects of yourself?

- Do you find yourself making self-deprecating statements, like "I'm not smart enough to …" or "I'm not good enough to …"?
- Do you ever punish yourself or deny yourself?
- Are you able to set boundaries with people that reflect your own moral and ethical standards and your own values and beliefs?
- Look in the mirror. How do you feel about yourself? Do you smile or frown?
- Where are you on the continuum of self-love?
- Are you appreciative and admiring?
- Are you critical and judgmental, or do you appreciate yourself just for who you are?
- Are you compassionate and loving toward this person you see?

IN THEIR OWN WORDS …

I've been practicing my self-hypnosis for four months and have lost almost forty pounds. I can do things without wheezing, and my joints have quit hurting. The area of my lifestyle where I see the biggest change is that I look in the mirror and *like* myself. I need to look like *me*. What pleases me the most is that I know now that I don't have to beat myself up. This program helped me change my attitude from negative to positive. It turned me from dark to light … my life is better.

ARIANA

If you are ambivalent, then ponder these questions further. Be honest with yourself. Have a discussion with yourself. Have an honest look at yourself. Don't just look at your body; look at your intellect, your spirit, your emotions, and your heart. Know this: By loving yourself, you appreciate yourself. If there is something you cannot accept about yourself, know that you can change that thought, and change it to create whatever you want, including your perfect weight.

How Does It Feel to Love Yourself?

Take a look at the following attributes. Are these familiar to you? This is how it will feel if you love yourself:

- You feel happy and accepting of your world, even though you may not agree with everything in it.
- You are compassionate with your shortcomings or less-than-perfect behaviors, knowing that you are capable of changing and improving.
- You thankfully appreciate compliments, and feel proud inside.
- You honestly view your faults, and gently accept them or learn how to change them.
- You enthusiastically accept all the good that comes your way.
- You honor your good qualities and the good qualities of everyone around you.
- You look in the mirror and smile (at least most of the time).

A LOVING PHILOSOPHY

Perhaps our bodies simply need to spread out in order to embrace all the love and wisdom we have gathered over the years.

Many confuse self-love with being arrogant and egotistical. Well, there are those who are so caught up in themselves that they earn the label of being self-centered and thinking only of themselves. We do not see that as a healthy self-love, but as a personality that is not well balanced in loving the self and loving others. It is not selfish to do things your way, but it *is* selfish to insist that everyone else does them your way also. The Dalai Lama says, "If you don't love yourself, you cannot love others. You will not be able to love others. If you have no compassion for yourself, then you are not capable of developing compassion for others." Dr. Karl Menninger, a psychiatrist, says it this way: "Self-love is not opposed to the love of other people. You cannot really love yourself and do yourself a favor without doing people a favor, and vice versa." We are talking about the healthiest form of self-love, which clears the way to accepting your greatest good.

Take a closer look at how you view your faults and blame yourself. Self-love and finding fault or blaming yourself are not at all compatible. If you suppress or deny loving yourself, you are at risk of paying too much attention to your faults, which is a form of self-loathing. You do not want to put attention on negative aspects of yourself, for by holding those thoughts in mind, you are giving them the mental energy that attracts that outcome or makes it real. As we suggested in chapter 2, put your conscious energy on the positive, not the negative. Self-love is positive energy. Blame, criticism, and faultfinding are negative energy.

Self-hypnosis can help you use your mind–body to create new and more loving thoughts and beliefs about yourself. It can help your mind–body make and accept changes in the patterns of thinking and feeling that have been with you for a long time, and that are not useful to you.

The trancework on the CD includes many positive hypnotic suggestions to shift your thoughts, feelings, and beliefs into alignment with having your perfect weight. A key target for these positive hypnotic suggestions is your innermost feeling of loving yourself. If your self-loving feelings are consistent with having your perfect weight, it will happen with greater ease. However, if you harbor resentment or guilt, or feel undeserving, these feelings work against loving yourself enough to believe and accept your perfect weight. Lucille Ball said it nicely: "Love yourself first and everything falls in line."

The hypnotic suggestions on the CD are instructions for change directed to the most "inner" level of mind-body or subconscious. But the "outer" changes in life activity must also occur. Many weight loss methods you have been using may seem to be too much work. We propose that by adopting an attitude that is without the emotional pressure associated with "having to," "good or bad," or "easy or difficult," without any judgment at all, the changes can be joyous. Yes, joyous. This makes the entire journey of making changes and of changing easier. The phrase "a labor of love" means that you love doing it so much that it is not a labor or obligation. The "labor" of preparing a family feast on a holiday, volunteering at a school or hospital, or shopping for a gift for someone very special can seem effortless. This is the attitude that will serve you in pursuing any weight loss methods. We encourage you to put yourself in the position of being loved. You are doing this for *you*. Loving yourself removes the work so you can enjoy your progress toward a lifestyle that supports your perfect weight. Think of some activity that you love to do. Imagine yourself doing that activity now. Notice that when you are doing something that you absolutely love to do, you feel wonderful and energized, and any effort is overshadowed by pleasure. What is happening at those times is that you view it as absolutely "loving what you are doing." At those times, we suggest that you also see this as "loving yourself doing it." Perhaps by directing more positive attitude toward loving yourself, you will find yourself loving what you are doing.

Lisa's Brimming Smile

When Lisa and Rick married, both were slim and enjoyed active lifestyles that included softball and aerobics classes at the local fitness center. When their first baby was born, Lisa had gained an extra fifteen pounds. By the time their second baby arrived three years later, she was forty pounds overweight. Overwhelmed by the demands of motherhood, she relied on quick frozen meals, canned foods, and fast food for the family table. Chronic sleep deprivation also kept her energy level low, and she could barely keep up with the toddlers. Rick, a promising young business executive, took on more and more responsibilities at work, climbing the "ladder of success," indulging in business lunches, and working late hours. He would return home late, collapse in front of the TV, and eat leftover pizza. The young couple accepted their frazzled lifestyle, but watched with dismay as their bodies grew old and tired beyond their years. Yet, they continued. When their oldest boy entered preschool, they became disturbed. Little Ricky seemed to be the target of every germ, and he began to miss many days of school. If that wasn't enough, he brought the germs home to little brother, mom, and dad, too. It seemed that all four of them were down with something the entire winter. The baby was colicky. In the spring, after a family bout with flu, Lisa's friend offered the name of a behavioral nutritionist who she said might be able to shed some light on the recurrent illnesses of Lisa's little boys.

At the first appointment, Lisa recounted the last four years of her family's lifestyle, culminating in the recent flu from which the little boys were still recuperating. They were tired, cranky, not sleeping well, and generally under the weather. With summer vacation just around the corner, Lisa was desperate to get her family back on track. The words of the nutritionist were very simple: Start feeding yourself and your family foods that are fresh and prepared at home. Start buying more fruits and vegetables, and create some easy recipes with brown rice and other grains. Learn to make simple and healthy dishes for your family. These words triggered Lisa to recall when she was a child about the age of her own little boys. She

THE SELF-HYPNOSIS DIET

fondly remembered her mom fixing big fruit salads with fresh pine-apple. She remembered delicious bowls of homemade soup and warm fresh bread. At that moment, Lisa knew what she wanted to make happen for her boys. And she *did* make it happen. About six months later, we received a phone call from Lisa. I could hear the smile brimming in her voice. "You can't believe the change in our family. Ricky has had only one cold in the last six months, we are all sleeping better, and the baby is happy and sleeping through the night. Four days a week, we take a family walk either after breakfast or after dinner. And guess what? I've lost thirty-five pounds, and I wasn't even dieting! I feel better than I've ever felt."

> Whatever you are doing, love yourself for doing it. Whatever you are thinking, love yourself for thinking it.
> THADDEUS GOLAS

MOTIVATION MAKER

Imagine your weight loss program to be just as enjoyable and effortless as any of these "labors of love": serving meals at a homeless shelter, reading to an elderly person, "big-brothering" an underprivileged child, volunteering at an animal shelter, providing a foster home for a parentless child, childbirth (perhaps one of the greatest labors of love!), and serving yourself, too. The more you give, the more you receive.

Giving Forth

Forgiveness is an important step in loving yourself. Whenever you forgive, you are "giving forth" or "letting go" of something you were holding within you. Let us be clear about this: forgiveness is only for you, not anyone else. It is not a form of accepting, condoning, or justifying someone else's actions. It is a process of letting go of a negative feeling that has stayed within you far too long. It is the letting go of any emotion or thought that might be a barrier between you and loving yourself and having what you want. Many of us are much more critical and much harder on ourselves than we are on others. When you hold on to thoughts of what you should or should not have done, you are not loving yourself. Instead, you are putting conscious energy into negative beliefs about yourself. Thoughts such as "I should have taken a walk yesterday" or "I shouldn't have eaten that second piece of pie" may also be seen as self-punishing. In some cases, punishing yourself, either through lack of eating or overeating, can even result in disregard for your health. By shifting your attention to self-appreciation, you move from the negative to the positive, which is much more conducive to self-loving. Writing in a journal about the healthy choices you make each day can promote self-love. By forgiving yourself and forgiving others, you release the emotional hold that past events may have had on you, and you make yourself available to love yourself. When you release the effects of past experiences by forgiving, you then experience a peace of mind and a peaceful relaxation in your body that help you accept your perfect weight.

You at the Head Table

Loving yourself also includes putting yourself first. To lose weight and achieve your perfect weight, *you* must come first. Therapist and writer Jean Fain wrote an article titled "The 'Yes, I Can' Diet," originally published in the September 2005 issue of *O: The Oprah Magazine*. She recalls a forty-nine-year-old mother who wanted to lose thirty-five pounds telling her, "I don't care enough about myself to care what I eat." She also didn't care about when she ate. She had no time for herself. Her life seemed to be in constant service to the demands of her husband, her daughter, her elderly mother, her business; they all came before her. She ate junk food despite the weight gain, took blood pressure medicine, and the thought of a diet was just too much, given her circumstances and her state of mind. With the help of her therapist, she

MOTIVATION MAKER

No blaming is allowed in the Self-Hypnosis Diet.
Give up all hope for a better past. Forgive, let it go, and shift into the spirit of acceptance. Accept the hypnotic suggestions that are offered during the trancework.

Guilt and regret are emotions that inhibit your self-love. Guilt is thought and feeling that occurs when you do something that you *know* is "wrong." Regret is the feeling that develops later, when you realize that you could have done it differently. For example, you can feel guilty for eating two pieces of cake that are forbidden by your diet. Or you can regret that you did not have the fruit plate instead of the cake. As you can see, they are pretty close, but not the same. The point we want to bring to your attention is that *there is no place for either guilt or regret when it comes to loving yourself.* They are both forms of blaming yourself. No blaming is allowed on the Self-Hypnosis Diet. Give up all hope for a better past. Forgive, let it go, and shift into the spirit of acceptance. Accept the hypnotic suggestions that are offered during the trancework.

BASIC RULES OF THE SELF-HYPNOSIS DIET

- No excuses
- No blaming
- No criticizing

This includes yourself, a piece of cake, a mother-in-law who pushes food at you, or anything else. Negative thoughts, ideas, and expressions are not allowed in your consciousness (or not for long anyway).

found time to listen to relaxing CDs, to get a massage, to read a book. In short, she found ways to put herself first and still tend to others without such a high cost to self. The article included an e-mail from her, twenty pounds lighter, stating, "I am not at my goal yet, but I know I will succeed." Self-love and putting yourself first go hand in hand. They are a winning combination. Any guilt you feel about putting yourself first can be dealt with by addressing your reasons for feeling guilty and then making choices to remove them. Do whatever it takes to clear your path to your perfect weight.

MOTIVATION MAKER
A Gratifying Food Journal
Consider buying a "specialized" journal. Write down which fruits and vegetables or whole grains you eat each day, or other healthy food choices you make. Reading your journal every evening will be an inspiration for the following day. Gloat about it.

Felicia's Holiday "Gift"

Felicia came home riddled with guilt. The pre-holiday season had a stranglehold on her once again as she shopped in preparation for their family tradition of Father Christmas' arrival with presents for all the little ones in their household. Even though she and her husband struggled to balance their bank account for just the basic expenses, Felicia had spent beyond their budget. As the holidays approached, using the "plastic" was just too tempting for her. Although the children delighted in all the presents, the expense put undue strain on the parents' relationship. Felicia resolved to remedy her tendency to spend too much money, relieve her guilty conscience, and focus on the blessings of her healthy and happy family. A caring friend

MOTIVATION MAKER

Four Ways to Banish Guilt

1. Use a talisman to banish your guilt "magically." Choose an object, such as an old vase, pot, box, or bag. Take your feelings of guilt and pretend you are putting those feelings into your talisman. Spend a few minutes contemplating that your feelings of guilt are now entirely inside that talisman. Go outside and use some type of ritual to remove the existence of that talisman and its contents: smash it with a hammer, burn it, or bury it. Feel the release and enjoy.

2. Write about your guilt in a special section of your journal. Write about the circumstances and those involved. Write about the feelings you had at the time. Write about your regrets. Write about the lessons you learned. Write about the changes you made, if any. Release those feelings onto the page and leave them there. Or even better, burn the pages in the fireplace and release those feelings upward into the air—gone, forever.

3. Talk to someone who loves you about your feelings of guilt. Expressing the feelings helps to release them.

4. Put yourself "on trial," and if found "guilty," accept a form of self-service as your "sentence." For example, maybe you canceled an invitation to visit with your adult child during a moment of bad temper. Feelings were hurt. Go apologize in person, even if it means a two-hour drive.

advised her to choose a talisman to represent her materialistic tendencies and her resulting feelings of guilt, and to plan a ritual to banish it all. One quiet afternoon, when her husband had taken the children to Central Park, Felicia found a colorful, glass holiday ornament stored in the closet. She spent a few minutes contemplating her materialism and guilt about overspending, and imagined placing it all inside the beautiful ornament. She took the talisman into the backyard, placed it under a tree, and with the back of a big spoon, ritually crushed the ornament into tiny sparkling bits that seemed to disintegrate into the soil. Magically, Felicia felt a great weight lifted from her shoulders and an overwhelming thankfulness for her healthy and happy family.

What Would You Like? What Do You Want?

Do you have a healthy self-image? There are many psychological tests that measure self-image, but our goal here is not psychotherapy. So let us just ask you, "Are you happy with the way you look?"

The question begs another question: "What changes would please you?" There is no room for blame, guilt, regret, or putting mental energy into negative feelings. The questions and choices are all about what you would like and what you want, followed by the thoughts, beliefs, and actions that bring those results about for you.

Do you feel your physical appearance affects how others treat you or feel about you? Unfortunately, the answer for everyone is "yes." Body-size stereotypes have been studied in much research. Studies have even shown that professional therapists who work with overweight individuals have biases. If you are overweight, you have felt the bias of others through glances, manners of speech, and the differences in behavior toward you and others of lesser size. Size-based discrimination may be hardest on children. And the bias that children have toward overweight individuals is significantly increasing. A study in 1961 documented that children had bias against overweight children. The research involved showing children drawings and asking them which they liked the least. The four drawings depicted children, including a child in a wheelchair, one with a disfigured face, one who might be called "normal," and an obese child. The drawing of the obese child was picked most often as the one they liked the least. This study was replicated with 458 fifth- and sixth-grade children in 2003. In the new study, the difference between how much they liked the "normal" child over the obese child was more than 40 percent greater than in 1961 (Janet Latner, Ph.D., and Albert Stunkard, M.D., *Obesity Research,* Vol. 13, No. 7, July 2005).

BELIEF BOOSTER

Intrinsic motivation ("from within," such as love, faith, health) is lasting motivation for weight loss. Extrinsic motivation ("from without," such as physical appearance, looking good for someone else) is fleeting motivation.

Other research shows that teens who reported being teased about their weight were more dissatisfied with their bodies, and considered or attempted suicide more often than their peers who did not report being teased about weight (Marla E. Eisenberg, Sc.D., *The Archives of Pediatric & Adolescent Medicine,* Vol. 157, No. 8, August 2003). In a study of 90,118 teens enrolled in the National Longitudinal Study of Adolescent Health, researchers found that those teens who were overweight were more likely to be socially isolated and on the outer edge of social networks than their normal-weight peers, and they had significantly fewer friendship invitations (Richard S. Strauss, M.D., *The Archives of Pediatric & Adolescent Medicine,* Vol. 157, No. 8, August 2003). These studies merely validate what any overweight person perceives in our culture. Overweight people do not need any reinforcement to dislike themselves or their self-image. The social and cultural biases and body-size stereotypes create painful emotions and may contribute to lower self-esteem and even poorer self-image.

Obviously, at the societal level, we need to do a better job of educating ourselves about what is important in valuing each person, and what is not. And we need to approach issues of obesity with a greater sensitivity to those who are overweight.

If you are having a tough time personally with others' glances and opinions about your body weight, use them to fuel your motivation to achieve a healthy body. Adopt the new mindset that every person and every remark is now a gift, not a curse. That is how you must treat them, as gifts. Each gift in the form of an opinion about your weight is a reminder that you love yourself, that you are moving toward your perfect weight, and that you are so much more sensitive and compassionate than they are. Terry Cole-Whittaker wrote a lovely book titled *What You Think of Me Is None of My Business*. The book title says it all, and is a wonderful instruction on how to deal with the perceptions of others.

MOTIVATION MAKER

Find a gift in your obesity, as a way to "gain" insight and "lose" weight.

Self-acceptance also affects how we love ourselves. When we can accept ourselves as we are, seeing ourselves clearly, we have a better foundation upon which to change ourselves. Here is an example that illustrates a bias (or former bias) one of us had about appearances and self-acceptance. In 1986, Dr. G. was in the very small town of St. Johann, Austria, on St. Rupert's Day. He went to the Catholic church for Sunday service. As he tells the story, the church was overflowing, and "since I didn't speak German, I spent much time people-watching. One woman, sitting many rows ahead of me, caught my attention so strongly that I could barely look away. My thought was that she was the most unattractive woman I had ever seen in my life. Her features were not disfigured, but they might as well have been. Everything about her physical appearance was very unattractive. The word 'ugly' came to mind. However, at one point during the service, the children who were present were invited to the front of the church. They lined up; there was some type of recognition or award ceremony taking place. As names were called, the respective parents came up to stand with their children. Two of the children were much more animated than the others. I later learned that they were of Vietnamese decent. Despite the ceremony being conducted by the priest, these two children were smiling and looking only toward their parent in the congregation. They seemed more than overjoyed. They were ecstatic. It was a sight to behold. When their parent's name was called, the ugly woman I had been looking at rose and joined the children in front of the altar. The children held her tightly; they clung to her with the most loving admiration I have ever witnessed. In those moments, she became the most beautiful woman I had ever seen. She was a very happy and proud single mother of two adopted refugees who adored her. The beauty that I then saw in her provoked an uncontrolled flow of joyful tears that return whenever I describe this scene. And something very special happened to me. It caused me to 'accept' that I had been living my life perceiving others as attractive or unattractive based solely on the physical attributes endorsed by our culture. I thought I was tolerant and nonjudgmental, but this experience allowed me to see myself and accept what I was doing. I did not like what I saw and immediately resolved to change. Self-acceptance can be magical, because once you truly accept who you are or what you are doing, you cannot help but experience a change into who you want to be. My relationship with others in the world has been transformed by that experience of self-acceptance." We invite you to accept yourself, your self-image, as it is right now.

How to Love Your Body

One of the reasons we talk so much about loving yourself is because that is where your healthy self-acceptance has to begin. If you do not love yourself now, even having the sexy looks of a Paul Newman or a Marilyn Monroe cannot give that to you. By the way, did you know that Marilyn Monroe wore a size 14?

Stand in front of a mirror and look at your body. Begin with your head and work down through each part of your body.

1. Recall some of the things this body part has done for you.
2. Tell it "thank you" for something specific that it did for you.
3. Continue to the next body part.
4. After reaching your feet and toes, go back to your head. Proceed down your body, telling each body part, "I love you."

You are on the way.

Praise the Body, Tom

The first words out of Tom's mouth were "I hate my body." He went on for ten minutes, telling us that he disliked most qualities about himself and speaking very disparagingly about his body. He then paused and said, "Listening to myself just now, it sounds like I hate myself." It sounded like that to us, too. We all knew that it was not his desire to be unhappy with himself; otherwise, he would not be seeking counseling and nutritional advice. We started simply by asking him to catch himself each time he began to speak about his body unfavorably. He was instructed to either say nothing at all or formulate a compliment to his body. The rules were to entirely eliminate self-criticism and blame, and to praise his body. We saw him a few weeks later in a follow-up session, and he was smiling. He told us how surprised he was to notice how frequently he referred to his body with insulting remarks, and how hard it was to say something nice. However, after the first week, he noticed his pattern changing, along with other changes. He told us that as he became more loving to his body in his mind, he began to notice changes in his behavior toward his body. Tom described improvements in food choices, taking the stairs at work because his body needed exercise, and cutting articles about self-care out of magazines and taping them to the mirror. He even wrote some affirmations on cards and taped them to his bathroom mirror. In our counseling sessions, we learned that Tom was the only boy in a family with five girls, and his sisters had teased him about being a "vulgar man" with hairy parts, burps, belches, and other unpleasant attributes that they felt distinguished him from the opposite sex. They meant no harm, but a part of him, as a young boy, accepted their sentiments as real. Tom's newfound love for his body opened the way for a very successful weight loss that ultimately allowed him to also discontinue his medications for blood pressure and cholesterol.

I am Me. In all the world, there is no one else exactly like me. Everything that comes out of me is authentically mine, because I alone chose it—I own everything about me: my body, my feelings, my mouth, my voice, all my actions, whether they be to others or myself. I own my fantasies, my dreams, my hopes, my fears. I own my triumphs and successes, all my failures and mistakes. Because I own all of me, I can become intimately acquainted with me. By so doing, I can love me and be friendly with all my parts. I know there are aspects about myself that puzzle me, and other aspects that I do not know—but as long as I am friendly and loving to myself, I can courageously and hopefully look for solutions to the puzzles and ways to find out more about me. However I look and sound, whatever I say and do, and whatever I think and feel at a given moment in time is authentically me. If later some parts of how I looked, sounded, thought, and felt turn out to be unfitting, I can discard that which is unfitting, keep the rest, and invent something new for that which I discarded. I can see, hear, feel, think, say, and do. I have the tools to survive, to be close to others, to be productive, and to make sense and order out of the world of people and things outside of me. I own me, and therefore, I can engineer me. I am me, and I am Okay.

VIRGINIA SATIR

BELIEF BOOSTER

Neutralize Your Negative Self-Talk

Each time you have a thought, observe it and neutralize it if it doesn't support your perfect weight.

Change "I just look at food and gain weight" to "I can eat anything I want and keep my perfect weight."

Change "Ice cream goes right to my hips" to "Ice cream is a food I enjoy occasionally."

CHAPTER 6

FEEDING FEELING

Whatever we plant in our subconscious mind and nourish
with repetition and emotion will one day become a reality.

EARL NIGHTINGALE

G race's naturally stunning beauty and charm earned her a full scholarship to a prestigious modeling school. She dropped out after six months as her weight ballooned to over two hundred pounds, where it remained for the next fifteen years despite persistent weight loss efforts.

Jack, fifty years old, has been overweight since high school, despite playing sports, doing regular exercise, and making numerous attempts at weight loss. Whenever his weight begins to drop, he feels fearful until he regains the weight.

Mary has gained and lost the same twenty-five pounds through her adult life. She even knows the pattern and triggers, yet she feels helpless to change them and lose the weight once and for all.

Alex is a very successful executive in a competitive computer industry, who constantly struggles with his weight. He works hard, earns a high income, and can multitask better than most, but cannot control the size of his waist.

Ted was CEO of an international resource corporation. His friends watched as he progressively moved from being a picture of health to a health risk due to excess weight gain.

Grace, Jack, Mary, Alex, and Ted are real cases we saw in therapy for weight loss using hypnosis. Like many others, these individuals once thought that eating and food were the problems causing their excess weight. This chapter is about what they learned to be the true culprit—the emotional mechanisms that control or influence eating and weight gain. We will look at how underlying emotional issues are expressed in ways that cause and maintain excess weight. We will explore the use of hypnosis to uncover the role of emotions and weight. We are not going to talk about eating disorders—such as anorexia, bulimia, and pica—or other compulsive behaviors. This chapter is about the most common ways in which our bodies can subconsciously gain weight and keep it on.

MOTIVATION MAKER

Hypnosis is designed to help you change. If you keep doing what you've done, you'll keep getting what you've got.

- Buy a limited membership at a fitness center, and hire a personal trainer for a few visits. You deserve it.
- Studies reveal that moderate physical training, such as walking, seems to be just as effective as more rigorous training, such as running. Start moving and start walking just fifteen minutes a day. As your fitness increases, gradually increase the time to one hour, five times a week.
- Dance. Sign up for lessons, or just turn on your favorite music and dance as if no one is watching.

The Mind–Body Mirror

Since these cases are from our mind-body medicine practice, let us briefly look at some of the typical ways that physical conditions are generated by the mind-body. There are many examples in which suppressed and repressed emotions find expression by manifesting as physical symptoms and conditions. Emotions and emotional conflicts that are not consciously acknowledged, expressed, or given voice can or will be expressed by the physical body.

Here is a very common example. When anger is not acknowledged and expressed, it may cause muscles in the head, neck, and shoulders to tighten and tense, which in turn creates a tension headache. This is the literal expression of something or someone that is a *pain in the neck*. Another person experiencing the same feelings of anger might be *burning up* over the situation, and experience heartburn, indigestion, or a fever. The skin is an organ that is highly responsive to emotions, and a condition of urticaria (hives) may erupt when there is someone *getting under their skin,* or *rubbing them the wrong way,* or when the person is *itching* to do or say something, or some emotion is *erupting to the surface.*

BELIEF BOOSTER

Hunger Signs

Pay attention to your feelings of true hunger. Most of us notice a growling stomach or a gnawing sensation that signals hunger. If you aren't certain whether you are hungry or not, you probably aren't. Thirst, fatigue, and boredom are often disguised as hunger. So have a tall glass of water, take a snooze, or turn on a great DVD the next time you want to eat but aren't actually certain if you're hungry.

Your emotions are your feelings, such as happy, sad, or angry. When emotions or feelings are not expressed, the mind–body will mirror them in creative ways. Therapeutically, metaphors help us decode and understand what the body is expressing. In chapter 1, we spoke about the subconscious or mind–body having its own language—a very literal one. A figure of speech or metaphor describing an emotional reaction such as "a pain in the neck" is literally expressed through muscle tension and headache, because the emotional frustration is not being expressed otherwise. This is a frequent experience, since many times it is not acceptable or advisable to acknowledge and express anger or other feelings. For example, if your supervisor embarrasses you or makes an unreasonable request, you could jeopardize your employment if you expressed your anger. Instead, you put it out of mind and go on to something else. *Putting it out of mind does not put it out of body.* As you will see in the examples of hypnosis used in therapy, emotions and emotional conflicts can be put out of mind, but not necessarily out of body. You can suppress emotions or repress them. Suppressing emotions is when you deliberately choose to not think about them. Repressing emotions happens when your subconscious does that for you without your having the benefit of choosing to do it yourself.

We would like to describe the difference between feelings and thoughts. Thoughts are ideas, beliefs, and judgments in your conscious or "thinking mind." Feelings or emotions are expressed physically in your body. They originate from a primitive area deep in the brain called the limbic system. Both thoughts and emotions are "things" in the sense that they are not *just in your mind.* They involve energy and chemistry, and they are transmitted physically and energetically through your nervous system and other pathways in your body. The chemical substances called neurotransmitters, such as serotonin, dopamine, noradrenaline, and acetylcholine, are the more common ones involved. In chapter 9, we will describe foods that influence the neurotransmitters making up or carrying the emotional energy of moods, as well as those influencing concentration, focus, mental energy, and sleep. If a person experiences mental sluggishness, he may notice more mental acuity if he includes oatmeal, nuts, and other choline-rich foods in his daily choices. Choline supports the functions of acetylcholine, which in turn supports memory and mental sharpness. For our purposes here, we want to emphasize that these emotional and cognitive responses and patterns are physically real and have been studied. If you are interested in this, you will enjoy Candace Pert's book *Molecules of Emotion* and her audio CD *Your Body Is Your Subconscious Mind*.

> Your key to happiness is not your perfect weight. Your perfect weight is a result of your happiness. Happiness is a feeling.

> We are emotions and emotions are us. Again, I can't separate emotions. When you consider that every aspect of your digestion, every sphincter that opens and closes, every group of cells that comes in for nourishment and then moves out to heal something or repair something, are all under the influence of the molecules of emotion, I mean, it's this total buzz.
>
> CANDACE PERT, PH.D., from *What the Bleep Do We Know!?*

Feelings or emotions include pain, fear, guilt, sadness, happiness, anger, joy, bliss, contentment, calm, anxiety, and loneliness. Notice that "bad" and "good" are not in the list of feelings. Even though we might say "I feel bad" or "I feel good," these are not emotions. These are judgments about what you feel, but they are not feelings. More properly, when you make these statements you actually mean "I feel badly" or "I feel well," which are ways to describe how you are feeling, not what you are feeling. Now here is the one worth remembering: "fat" is not a feeling. Even though people say, "I feel fat," "fat" is *not* a feeling. When someone says they are "feeling fat," it is a statement about a *sensation*, such as feeling satisfied, stuffed, full, or beyond full. You may be thinking, "Why the big deal over the choice of words? I know what I mean when I say that." The reason we emphasize this is that your feelings and your words about your feelings are a part of your beliefs about yourself, and when you hold these in consciousness or speak them aloud, they are direct messages to your subconscious. Your mind-body hears it all, and even long after it is out of your mind (awareness), it is not out of your body's mind. You will want to choose carefully what your mind-body is to believe and expect about your weight and what and how you *feel* about it—for it will literally mirror it.

IN THEIR OWN WORDS ...

In two weeks, the Self-Hypnosis Diet has relieved me of my obsession with mindless eating, and has allowed me to increase my energy, decrease my portions, and start on my way to my perfect weight. I wish the Self-Hypnosis Diet had been around before I ever started dieting!

ERIN

Saving Grace

Something happened to Grace that caused her to miss out on her modeling school scholarship. She came to our office and expressed the desire to use hypnosis to help her lose weight. She described many different trials of weight loss methods that had been unsuccessful. Whenever she did lose weight, it would return. She felt that there was "something" keeping her from losing weight. In taking her history, we learned that she was thirty-six years old, married with three children ages nine, seven, and five. Her weight had been consistently over two hundred pounds for about fifteen years. She grew up in the Midwest in a good family, and had three sisters. Grace described herself as the only one in her family with a weight problem. When questioned about her weight history, she would only say that she "ate too much." After completing a comprehensive psychological and nutritional assessment, we proceeded to teach her about hypnosis. When she felt comfortable enough to proceed, we began with an induction method like the ones on the CD with this book. Grace relaxed easily into a trance state, wherein she was comfortably absorbed in her thoughts and ideas of a relaxing and pleasant scene. As she imagined being on vacation with her family, I offered hypnotic suggestions to her subconscious about letting her have insight into the purpose or function of her excess body weight. Within a few minutes, she looked stressed, and I asked her to describe what she was experiencing as she continued in trance. She described riding a train and being the first to arrive at the modeling college. The administration office was closed, but a friendly janitor helped her with her suitcases and unlocked the door to her assigned dorm room. She was becoming increasingly tearful and tense as she continued speaking. I assured her that she could interrupt the trance at any time or she could proceed more slowly and comfortably, and I reminded her that she knew she was in our office *now* as she was remembering something that took place *then,* fifteen years ago. Through her tears, she described the friendly janitor returning later that night, letting himself into her room and raping her. The memory of this experience was quite tiring and emotionally draining for Grace. Talking with her after the trancework, I learned that it had been almost fifteen years since she had thought about that experience. She had forgotten it. Initially, she chose to put this out of her mind, to suppress this memory, but it was put out of her mind so well that she had even forgotten that she forgot it. It was repressed. She also said that this was the only time and place that she had ever spoken to anyone about the experience.

We spent another session talking about her experience in modeling college, and I asked her to bring in some photographs from that period. We used the photographs to help her remember events so that she could talk about them in the safety of therapy. She related that during the first six months in college her weight gradually increased, and she was nervous, fearful, ashamed, depressed, and sleep-deprived. She did not speak about the rape with anyone, and went home to marry her high school sweetheart. He had always accepted her for herself, and her weight was truly not an issue with him. Our counseling sessions revealed that the purpose of her excessive body weight was as a form of protection. Her weight safely controlled her attractiveness so that she was protected from being the target of another sexual assault. Once she acknowledged, expressed, and processed the experience and emotions (fear, shame), Grace's weight loss program was very effective in reducing her size to where she felt happy and safe. In her case, we see that the subconscious was serving a function and there was a purpose for the excess weight. It protected her and allowed her to feel safe. Although there was a time when she was pleased that others found her attractive, the assault created a fear that became associated with being attractive. After examining these feelings and getting rid of the fear, she was free to release her extra weight and feel safe when she felt attractive.

Jack Eats to Live

The case of fifty-year-old Jack was different, and illustrates another common emotional conflict. He was very active in sports throughout his life and exercised regularly, but would frequently overeat just enough to maintain excessive weight. He was only twenty to twenty-five pounds overweight, and despite wanting to lose those pounds, he described feeling "fearful" whenever he actually lost weight. When I took his history, he reported only one event that was "scary." He told me that when he was ten years old, he had a serious illness that caused him to stay at home, out of school, for one year. He thought it was some type of tuberculosis. He told me that the illness was in the past, and he felt that it now had no influence or effect on his life. We used hypnosis to revisit that time and let him see if it had any relationship to his weight problem. While in the daydream-like state we call trance, Jack described having his bed in the living room because his bedroom had begun to feel like a hospital room. He liked being in the living room because that was where all the action in the home took place. While still in trance, he began to laugh as he described the scene, and told me that he used to think that if he stayed in the living room, he would be able to keep "living." He also recalled seeing his parents' fear over his loss of weight and frail body. They seemed to relax only after he had eaten enough. After the trancework, we discussed his perceptions of his parents' fear that he was so thin he would die. In the 1930s through the 1950s, this was a common fear of parents whose children were stricken with serious illness. Jack talked to his body and verbalized his now-adult rationale with his body. He wrote some affirming statements about his health and vitality on cards and kept them handy to read throughout the day. He reprogrammed his mind-body to accept his vitality and release the weight. In addition to losing excess weight, he also discovered that his nervousness about going to the doctor's office ceased.

In Jack's case, his mind-body protected him from the perceived threat of death that was associated with a thin body. The ten-year-old Jack did not have the intellectual sophistication to understand his parents' concern and worry. His mind-body performed the functions necessary to save his life (i.e., gain weight)—or that is the way the ten-year-old's subconscious perceived it.

In both Grace's and Jack's cases, we see that the memory of an emotionally charged event was managed purposefully by the mind-body. At the time, Grace felt helpless to do anything about the sexual assault. The twenty-year-old modeling student felt ashamed and afraid, and she kept the experience of sexual trauma to herself. Gradually, this event was buried in memory and she no longer had access to it. All she knew was that modeling college did not work out, she did not like the school experience, she gained weight, and she went home, where she felt safe and married her closest friend and sweetheart. She recovered the repressed memory by asking her subconscious to share any information with her that would help her release the weight. In Jack's case, he knew he had a serious illness as a child, but did not remember enough about the actual details that would allow him to see that his mind-body was still serving a purpose for him with the excess weight. Remember, ideas, thoughts, and beliefs can be out of mind, but not necessarily out of body.

Comfort Pudding

Let us look at another case that illustrates another common emotional theme played out by the mind-body in weight problems. Mary described a lifetime of gaining and losing what she called "the same twenty-five pounds of weight." When we took her history, she said that her weight problems began when she went to college, and recurred with each geographic move and with each relationship change. At age thirty-six, Mary was well educated and made wise choices about her food and eating behavior. She was successful in all areas of her life and was baffled over why she could not be successful in losing weight. She had read some books about hypnosis and wanted to use it to tell her body to lose the weight. Mary went into a relaxed state of trance easily. We offered hypnotic suggestions to help her discover if there were any obstacles or barriers to her weight loss. That is, we asked her subconscious if there was a reason for regaining and keeping the weight that she wished to lose. Images of fourth grade come to her mind. Mary described a warm spring day when she was nine years old, walking home from elementary school. Arriving home, she pulled out the key her mother gave her that morning so she could let herself into the house. Mary's mother had left her job as a nurse when Mary was born. This was the first day of her mother's return to her nursing career, and this was the first time Mary had come home to an empty house. In my office, Mary began to cry as she remembered feeling so lonely without her mom there to greet her in the kitchen, even though she knew her mom would be home in less than an hour. She walked through the house, feeling a mixture of numbness and loneliness. She described the physical sensation of being "empty" in the middle of her tummy. Back in the kitchen, she found a note on the kitchen table with her name on it. It said, "Hi, Honey, I will be home soon. I put some pudding in the refrigerator for you. Love, Mommy." Mary was now half laughing, half crying as she told me that she could even taste the comfort of that vanilla pudding right now, here in the office. Later, she wrote out a chronology of her weight and the association to geographic moves, job changes, and relationship changes. She saw her pattern of eating sweets (such as pudding and other desserts) during the times she needed to fill the emptiness when lonely or when missing what or whom she left whenever she moved. Mary found what she needed to change, so food did not have to fill the emotional emptiness anymore.

> ## MOTIVATION MAKER
> *What nourishes you?*
>
> Here are a few ideas we hear from clients: reading poetry, fresh flowers, playing the guitar or flute, watching a good DVD, feeding the birds, silence, walks in nature, music, artwork, peace and quiet, time with a friend, playing with a cat or dog or other pet. Add your own favorite "nourishment" to this list, and use one the next time you aren't hungry but are reaching for the refrigerator door.

One of us presented a paper on using hypnosis to treat obesity at the American Society of Clinical Hypnosis' annual scientific meeting. In it, we explained that the emotional reasons for weight gain and retention fell into three groups. Approximately one-third of patients had a history of sexual trauma (similar to Grace); one-third had a serious illness, hospitalization, or crisis in which parents feared their child would die (similar to Jack); and one-third had an experience of feeling empty or left alone, and food became the emotional comfort used throughout life (like Mary). We have found these three groupings to be fairly common in many of the cases that we see in clinical practice. Most important, when individuals recover or have the opportunity to acknowledge and express their feelings, no matter from how long ago, they can release the weight they want to lose.

Waist Not

Emotions and the messages they express in the mind–body do not have to be "traumatic." Alex, a successful executive, is a good example of how stress and emotions affect weight. When he came to our office, he was frustrated that he could be successful with everything in his life except his weight. He gave numerous examples of business success, personal achievements, and a capacity to work eighty hours per week. He said, "When it comes to my weight, I *feel* like a failure." During the hypnosis session, we explored the possibility of any underlying emotional conflicts. We found none. What we did find was Alex's frustration about feeling like a failure. We suggested that he create a new *feeling* to replace the feeling of failure. Despite his history of achievements, Alex had great difficulty replacing the feeling of failure. He argued that "as long as my waist is over thirty-six inches, I feel fat, and that makes me feel like a failure." Using self-hypnosis, he was able to *relax this feeling* and let himself imagine that his waist was thirty-four inches. In his imagination, he could see a "34 waist" label in his pants, and he could also imagine himself in a fine men's clothing store, trying on expensive trousers that were size 34 waist and admiring his image in a three-panel mirror. But most importantly, Alex was able to eventually *feel* himself wearing a 34 waist, which was a feeling of *being* a 34 waist. The feeling he imagined allowed him to feel successful, as if his weight were less and he had already achieved his goal. He practiced and rehearsed this imagery and feelings in his mind several times per day for three weeks. When he returned to the office, he described discovering many changes in his eating behavior that seemed to occur automatically. Among those changes, he was now eating a healthy breakfast with wonderful food choices; he forgot to eat the usual on-the-run pastries at his work; his alcohol consumption diminished significantly; and when he was full, he stopped eating, and left the uneaten portion without any guilt about not cleaning his plate. His waistline shrank two inches in three weeks, and he said, "It is working. I know my waist is shrinking, I can *feel* it." Why did his waist and weight change now and not before, when he was aggressively trying to lose weight? It was happening now because he could believe it and he could *feel* it. The feeling or emotion was the key ingredient. When you use the CD with this book, put your feelings to work for you, too. The message we learn from Alex's case is that just as you choose the "belief," you can also choose the "feeling" that you want your mind-body to act out for you.

The Image of Success

Ted was fifty-eight years old. Apart from an annual physical examination, he rarely saw his physician. His doctor referred him to mind-body medicine because his health was declining rapidly with increasing weight, and with no apparent physical disease as a cause. In fact, his recent weight gain was causing a great risk of heart disease, with higher cholesterol, higher blood pressure, and blood sugar levels that were nearing diabetes. When Ted came to the office, he seemed resigned to being ill. He was accepting the weight gain and his symptoms too well. He did not seem to be bothered by his condition or very motivated to act on his own behalf. However, he did follow his doctor's order and came to see us. His history was insightful. Two years earlier, his board of directors had voted to remove him as president of the manufacturing company he had built up over the previous twenty years. Although he received a severance package to ease the economic hardship, the damage to his ego was irreparable. He had all the symptoms of depression: poor sleep, weight change, poor appetite, social withdrawal, fatigue, loss of interest in pleasurable activities, and a feeling of detachment. Even with a very poor appetite, he had gained over thirty-five pounds. His doctor prescribed an anti-depressant medication, which only caused further weight gain. Ted told me that he did not have the energy to do any exercise, let alone job-seeking to find new employment. He proved to be an excellent hypnotic subject, and quickly learned how to select thoughts, ideas, beliefs, and imagery that gave his subconscious a message to restore his identity. In the language of medical hypnosis, these are termed ego-strengthening suggestions. Quite simply, they are positive statements intended to boost confidence, self-image, and positive feelings about oneself. For the time being, he chose first to tackle his weight, which was undermining his health. He literally made "losing weight" his new full-time job— and he did it well. He threw himself into the project of learning everything that he could about weight, diets, and exercise. Ted treated his weight loss as "work activities" to restore his feelings of self-worth. The more he did to feel better about his weight, the better he felt about himself as a person. He lost weight, gained a new position in a completely different field, and regained control of his life. Those around him watched his transition from a successful CEO to a depressed man with increased weight and poor health, then back to a vital and happy person again. Ted was aware that the people around him credited his weight loss to his many physical activities, such as walking and swimming, and his learning about wholesome nutrition. However, he credited the mental work of imagery and affirmations with self-hypnosis as the key ingredient that made it all happen.

Buried Emotions

As you can see from these case studies, feelings can work for you or against you. Sometimes you may be aware of the emotions that affect eating and weight, and sometimes they are out of mind. Emotional conflicts can be related to intense trauma or simply be feelings that persist without our awareness of their effect. In either case, the feelings or emotional conflicts can be buried, and *no amount or type of food can effectively keep them buried without a consequence*. In your experience with self-hypnosis, it is important to choose the feelings you want to have about yourself, your weight, your body, and the activities that will help you achieve your perfect weight. It is equally important to open your mind to see *what* emotional conflicts may have become patterns of eating and lifestyle that support excess weight.

Physical Hunger—Mouth Hunger—Emotional Hunger

Physical hunger is the sensation that your body creates to get the nutrients it needs to live. You feel this need to eat to satisfy the physical body, to regulate and balance blood sugar levels, and to fuel your body's vital energy and engine. Mouth hunger is the desire you might feel to *keep eating* after you are satisfied, because something tastes so good. Emotional hunger is the need to eat to feel better *emotionally*. And as we saw, you may not even be aware that your subconscious or mind–body is creating a desire to eat for an emotional reason.

If you feel that it is not easy to determine which type of hunger you are feeling, you are not alone. Most of us grew up in a culture

MOTIVATION MAKER

Seven Ways to Lose It Fast

1. Every time you have a sweet treat, have a serving of vegetables.
2. Use smaller dishes. Research shows that we consume less when we drink from smaller glasses, eat from smaller plates, and ladle from smaller bowls.
3. Experiment with exotic foods. We usually eat less and slower when consuming unfamiliar foods, especially unfamiliar ethnic foods.
4. Snack on foods that are more laborious to prepare: nuts or edamame in the shell, seeded watermelon.
5. Know that you can always eat all the vegetables that you want.
6. Start your meals off with foods that are high in water, like clear soups and salads (with an olive oil and vinegar dressing).
7. When you are two-thirds through with your plate of food, put down your knife and fork. Spend ten minutes lingering, savoring the texture, flavor, and aroma of the meal, listening to the music, watching the flickering candle, continuing the gentle dinner conversation. After the ten minutes, think about your body. Is it satisfied? Are you full? Are you craving anything more? You may find that you are satisfied. Isn't that interesting? There is a very real phenomenon happening here. It takes about ten to twenty minutes for the brain to register fullness before we stop eating. That time is about all that separates us from being satiated to becoming uncomfortably full. A lot of calories can be packed down in those ten minutes.

that produced mixed messages about what our bodies feel and need. Here is an example. When you were little, were you encouraged to eat all of your food, to *clean your plate?* We would be surprised if you did not get this instruction growing up. But what did that message do to your ability to stay in tune with the signals that you body gives you about hunger? The admonishment to *clean your plate* teaches that even if you are not hungry, do not listen to your body, just eat everything on your plate. No wonder your ability to decipher your body's hunger signals gets confused with other signals.

Unconscious Eating

In addition to eating to satisfy hunger, you may have learned to multi-task while eating. That is, you can be eating and actually be unaware that you are eating. Have you ever experienced eating while reading a book or watching television or driving a car, and discover that you ate most of the meal and did not realize it until the food was almost gone? Or have you been engaged in conversation with someone while eating or even on the phone while eating and discover that you paid more attention to the conversation than to eating, tasting, or feelings of fullness? The point here is that by staying in tune with the signals and sensations of your body, you can stay in better control of the *feelings* that cause you to eat as well as those feelings that let you know when to stop eating.

The Emotional Continuum

We would like to present the idea of an emotional continuum, where one end is negative emotions and the opposite end is positive emotions. On the negative end are the feelings of guilt, shame, resentment, anger, hate, and fear. At the positive end of the continuum are happiness, bliss, joy, compassion, contentment, peace, and love. In regard to the effects of emotions, we would like you to think of them as either positive or negative, with the negative end called fear, and the positive end called love. Reduce each of the emotions to its representative effect of promoting either fear or love. When you identify the respective emotions and their effects as fear or love—one or the other—it will be easier for you to choose the ones you want and to release the ones you do not want. *Eating for emotional reasons has, at its core, the attempt to get rid of fear.* By choosing the positive, you produce the favorable conditions for happiness, which nourishes your perfect weight. Associating your eating with the positive emotions (love) is one way of unlearning the negative patterns of eating and treating food as love. It is fine to love your food, but do not make food a substitute for love and the other positive emotions. Challenge and erase the negative emotions (fear) with what they require, which is *not* food.

Every time you have an emotion or are about to eat, check in with the emotional continuum line in your head.

The Antidote to Stress

Just as our responses to emotions can create unhealthy eating patterns, such as excess snacking and unhealthy food choices, so can our responses to stress. With repetition, these patterns become lifestyle habits that cause weight problems. Stress can have many effects on health and weight. Some of the effects of stress are immediate and direct, such as the increase in blood pressure when your shoelace snaps as you race to an appointment. Your sympathetic nervous system can automatically prepare you to fight for your life, run for your life, or just freeze. Any threat, real or imagined, physical or psychological, can turn on the "fight–or–flight" response. Although this mechanism was intended to be our lifesaving defense, it is inappropriate for our civilized world. Our prehistoric ancestors needed a sympathetic response of fight-or-flight to survive and find food rather than *become* food. Today, most of the threats that turn on this physical defense or alarm system are psychological in nature. The fear of being embarrassed when speaking in front of a group is a very common stress that can lead to anxiety and panic attacks. Embarrassment is a threat to the ego, not the physical body.

It does not matter if the threat is real or imagined, physical or psychological; your body has learned many patterns of response. We refer to the negative body responses as "stress" or "stressors." Actually, any change is a form of stress. Anything that causes your body to make changes in order to adapt is a form of stress. That is, stress is "forced adaptation." Researchers have studied the range of stressful events and related them to illness. The relationship between stress and health is now accepted. Some stresses are useful and some can be harmful. *What is important to know is that the antidote to stress is relaxation.* You cannot be anxious and relaxed at the same time because they are two distinctively different physiological states. By learning to achieve peace of mind, or relaxation, you can neutralize the effects of stress.

Comfort or Nourishment?

You may now have an awareness of how stress affects your weight. For most individuals, stressful events or negative responses to those events can lead to excessive drinking or eating and unhealthy choices in food or behavior. Perhaps you have a special food that comforts you when you are stressed, frustrated, angry, or sad. We have had patients who can tell us which food comforts anger, which food comforts sadness, or which food they use as a reward or treat when they are upset or stressed. Certain food cravings may be more associated with emotional needs than with nutritional needs. One clue to identifying the foods that have become associated with emotional needs is to look at the foods or dishes that your parents fed you to "make you feel better." You can think of such comfort foods as medicine and self-medication. You can tell if you are using food this way by looking at your satiation or satisfaction. That is, if eating a reasonable amount does not satisfy your hunger, it may not have been *food* that you needed. Obviously, this is an unhealthy and inappropriate use of food in response to stress. Rather than continue to eat, stop, take a breath, and look at other things you might need.

We must also say that there *is* a time and place to love our food for all that it gives us. The famous chef Paul Prudhomme says it well in talking about his cooking: "We have a responsibility as citizens to do what we can for each other. It makes people happy. They eat it, and when they see me later, they want to hug me, to touch me, because Louisiana food is emotional food. It has a lot of flavor to it. You put it in your mouth in bad times and it makes you feel good." It is not bad to view food this way—it is only detrimental when not viewed this way in moderation. There is no need to label all our "comfort foods" as "bad," for neither the food nor the comfort is bad. It is only when we are unaware of what we are doing and why, that a problem is created or overlooked. The important things to be mindful of are our choices and self-control, so that we achieve and maintain a healthy body.

Journaling Exercise:

• List your comfort foods.
• Become aware of the times when you turn toward your comfort foods.
• Are you turning toward your comfort foods to enjoy them or to avoid an emotion?

BELIEF BOOSTER
Past-Life Effects

We are frequently asked if one's weight problem is a result of a past-lifetime experience. Without the ability to validate or corroborate the events of a previous lifetime, we can only speculate on the question of past lives. Our preference is to focus attention on this lifetime, as there are ample lessons to learn from it. However, there are individuals who believe that in a previous life they experienced starvation, which created a tendency in the present life to store food and gain weight. We have no way to authenticate the historical validity of this, but we can say that beliefs about starvation, or fear of starvation, can certainly lead to weight gain. Whether imagined or historically valid, beliefs can manifest as a result. Perhaps you have had many past lives, with many lessons in those lives. We propose that you select whatever beliefs will best serve your interests and realize your goals in *this* lifetime.

Finding Out the Answers

One way to manage stress-related eating and emotional hunger is to talk about it. Talking makes you more mindful and stimulates your subconscious to answer some of your questions. You can also use your self-hypnosis to go into trance and ask your subconscious those questions. Be patient, for the answer does not come as a trumpet blaring in your ear. Your subconscious is gentle and provides more of an intuitive knowing or inner wisdom. Also, answer these two questions for yourself: What do you feel when you are physically hungry? What do you feel when you are emotionally hungry?

The very best way to avoid feeding your feelings is to have a better, more effective way to manage stress. We can think of none better than relaxation and peace of mind. The calming peace of mind you learn to achieve with self-hypnosis from this book and CD may be the most powerful antidote to stress you discover. We cannot emphasize enough the importance of peace of mind and relaxation when looking for a way to remove food as a stress-relieving medicine in your life.

MOTIVATION MAKER

Numbing with Food

If you "numb" yourself from "feeling" by eating, you do not remove or alleviate the feeling; you only disconnect from it temporarily. The feeling will come back until you acknowledge it. Remember this: if you numb yourself from any single feeling, you have numbed yourself from *all* feelings, negative and positive.

You Can't Eat Enough ...

The best reason for eating is to satisfy hunger and obtain vital nourishment and energy. Other good reasons include the pleasures of eating, savoring the tastes and aromas, and social sharing among family and friends. There are many poor reasons for eating, including easing guilt, suppressing anger, absolving shame, filling an emotional emptiness, lessening anxiety and panic, and overcoming boredom, among a myriad of emotional reasons. Becoming aware of these motivators, along with the fact that you can't eat enough food to effectively suppress stress and emotions, will help you enjoy food and keep your healthy weight.

A Word about the Trancework

The trancework on the CD that accompanies this book includes suggestions for learning about any emotional barriers and factors influencing your weight. By discovering and understanding the relationship between eating, food, and emotions, you will be able to make healthier choices for yourself and pursue the removal of those barriers. If you feel you would like additional help with any emotional issues involved with your weight, please contact a counselor or attend a support group, begin journaling, and read relevant books (see Further Reading and Resources). Follow through on getting all the help you desire. Once you remove any emotional obstacles, you are free to enjoy a love affair with food.

CHAPTER 7

NOURISHING YOUR LOVE AFFAIR WITH FOOD

When one has tasted watermelon
he knows what the angels eat.
MARK TWAIN

D oes a love affair with food sound like something luscious and romantic, or does it sound like a head-on collision with weight gain? What kind of relationship would you like to have with food and eating? In your personal relationships, there are two options: you can choose to be in a relationship with a person, or you can elect to be "single" or "unattached." Even if someone else chooses to be in a relationship with you, you have the option to decline or run away. You don't have that option with eating. You cannot remove yourself from food and eating any more than you can dismiss air and breathing from your life. Since your food cannot make the choices about its relationship with you, you must do the choosing. You cannot escape it. This question will always be valid: What kind of relationship would you like to have with food and eating?

We know individuals who tell us that they hate to eat and find it a nuisance to even bother with it, preferring instead to take a pill if one were available. We also know people who do not own a stove and have no intention to cook or learn how. Everyone has the freedom to decide what relationship they would like to have with food. But since you are reading this book, it is apparent that we have something in common. Like us, you may like to eat and want to enjoy food. In fact, we can choose to indulge ourselves in a passionate love affair with food and still enjoy our perfect weight.

> ### IN THEIR OWN WORDS ...
> I have just started the Self-Hypnosis Diet. However, it is already having a positive effect on my way of thinking and on my stress as well. I have tried other diet aids, but really believe that this will be the healthy, successful way to go! Thank you!
> ROBERT

You Can Eat Anything You Want and Keep Your Perfect Weight

At sixty years of age, we (the authors) find that *we can eat anything we want and keep our perfect weight.* This ability seems more real to us than anything else. Let us repeat this, because it really does capture the essence of our relationship to food. We can eat anything we want—loving every bit—and keep our perfect weight. It is true for us, and it can also be true for you.

> Eating well is not about dieting, but a life choice. Adopting a healthy lifestyle through food should never leave us feeling deprived. I think most of us agree that eating is one of life's greatest pleasures ...
> ROSIE DALEY, *The Healthy Kitchen* (Andrew Weil, M.D., co-author)

It Seems That Way, So It Is That Way

Here is how it is done. By creating a healthy lifestyle and a relationship with our food that produces the results or perfect weight we want, it *seems* like we can eat anything we want and keep our perfect weight. If it *seems* that way to us, it is very real to us. It is our reality. It is the reality we live in. Now, if you examine our lifestyle and relationship to food, you will see that we pay attention to what we purchase, cook, and consume, so that we get the results we want. Remember what we said earlier: there are no mistakes, only unwanted results. We are constantly fine-tuning our lifestyle so that we can *eat anything we want and keep our perfect weight.* Not only do we make wise choices about food (lots of fresh vegetables, fruits, and whole grains), we eat normal portion sizes, we move our bodies, and there are many foods that we do *not* eat because they produce unwanted results. The bottom line is this: we pay attention to creating a lifestyle that produces the results we want for a healthy and happy body that is our perfect weight. Within this lifestyle, we are wonderfully adjusted to the habits and patterns that reward us with that healthy, happy body. Our lifestyle is so rewarding that we love it, and to us it truly seems as if *we can eat anything we want and enjoy our perfect weight.* If we can do this, so can you. A good portion of our life revolves around food, and we may even eat more and *enjoy* eating more than you do right now because we do it without guilt or negative emotions. We do not say these things to boast or separate ourselves from you, but rather so you will see that it is possible for *you* to enjoy a lifestyle in which it seems that you can eat what you want and have your perfect weight. What we propose is not a dieter's or restricted eater's lifestyle by any means. It truly is a loving relationship with food and eating.

You Make It Happen

Luck is not involved in having a healthy, loving relationship with food or anything else. But as anyone who has fallen in love knows, there is a special magic to being in a loving relationship. There is a magic that focuses your energy and uses your love to overcome any obstacle powerfully. The *magic* or energy that makes this happen is in your choices about what you want, or what motivates you, what you choose to believe, and what you expect. As we discussed in chapter 2, these basic ingredients cause other things to happen in your reality; for your perfect weight, this means wise food choices, exercise, and a lifestyle that produces the results you want. Another ingredient in your new relationship with food is your intention and attention. "Intention" is the mental idea of what you want. "Attention" is the focus or energy you place on what you are doing that will give you the results that you want. For example, you *intend* to eat just enough to be comfortably full, and not overstuffed. Your *attention* focuses on chewing each bite mindfully and slowly, and noticing when your body has had enough food. A healthy and loving relationship requires both your intention and your attention to produce the results you desire.

To nourish your healthy love affair with food and eating, let's take a look at the parallel to a healthy marriage or partnership. Bear with us here, for there are some very useful insights that you can draw upon for your loving relationship with food and eating. In your relationship with food, we will primarily look at the elements of selection, which include homogamy, complementarity, and trust. These are the same concepts or filters involved in a healthy, successful relationship or marriage.

First, we would like to entertain the principle of "residential propinquity" which says that what or who is closest to you has a better chance for selection. Or simply put, you are more likely to meet and fall in love with someone near you than with someone who lives in another city, another state, or another country. Similarly, locally grown foods are easier to love. Locally grown foods are fresher and tastier, and hold greater nutrient energy than food that was grown three thousand miles away and processed to last a long journey and to have a long shelf-life. Select what is near you, foods that come from where you live. Farmers' markets are one of the matchmakers in your love affair with food.

Homogamy

One filter in creating a relationship involves homogamy, which means similar interests and values. You are more likely to meet and fall in love with someone if you mingle with people who share similar interests and values. For example, if you enjoy art museums, you are more likely to find a compatible partner if you enroll in an art class than if you mingle with people at a beach volleyball competition. The same is true with food. If you want your perfect weight, you are more likely to achieve that goal if you surround yourself with foods that support healthy weight, such as fresh fruits and vegetables and whole grains, rather than with foods that are not compatible with your perfect weight, such as doughnuts, pizza, and French fries. We will give you all the nutritional information you need in chapter 9.

As in a relationship where you discover that the other person likes the things that you like, you may view your relationship with food as a mutual interest between you and your food. You love the foods that give you the perfect body weight, energy, health, and vitality, and those foods lovingly nourish you and your body. By eating foods that you love and that are healthy, you will enjoy eating in a new way.

BELIEF BOOSTER

In *The Little Book of Bleeps* by Betsy Chasse, Dr. Masaru Emoto presents research on water and ice crystals that suggests that thoughts and words directed toward water affect the water molecules. Loving thoughts and words create perfectly formed and beautiful ice crystal molecules. Hateful, angry thoughts and words produce deformed ice crystal molecules. Perhaps the age-old ritual of blessing food before eating it has more merit than we ever imagined. It is interesting, too, the implication that this might have for our bodies, considering that healthy humans are 50 to 65 percent water. As the man in the subway pondered in the movie *What the Bleep Do We Know!?*, "Makes you wonder, doesn't it ... If thoughts can do that to water ... Imagine what our thoughts do to us."

Complementarity

This is the filter where the differences between partners enhance the relationship. The differences you each bring to the relationship can now serve each other's needs and make the relationship stronger. In a partnership, it can be that one partner likes to do yard work and the other dislikes it. One likes to manage the finances, pay the bills, and write the checks, while the other partner gets a stomachache when they see the money fly out of the checking account each month. The differences complement the partners because each one serves the needs of the other. In your love affair with food, you can let your food provide you with protein, carbohydrates, and oils that you cannot manufacture yourself. And in turn, you give your food the body movements that burn the calories and convert the inherent food energy into a walk through a lovely park. Your dinner gives you a symphony of exquisitely tasteful treats and pleasures. Through your sleep that night, your body absorbs the nutrients during digestion for healthy cells, energy, and vitality. The next morning, you take your body for a walk or to a yoga class, or give it a workout that moves the absorbed nutrients to where they can now give you the perfect weight that you want. Seeing clearly what good benefits food provides can enhance your relationship with food. Next time you are eating, think of how much the food will nourish your body, and your perfect weight.

Trust

All loving relationships must be founded on trust. Trust is not "hit or miss," nor does it happen automatically. Trust requires intention and attention to make it happen regularly so that it becomes a habit. Remember, intention is the mental idea of what you want. Attention is the energy placed on what you are doing that will give you the results you want. You must be able to trust yourself in choosing foods that will give you the result you want. Food must not just satisfy hunger; it must also create the body weight you desire and emotional well-being. Your food must not betray you. Foods that betray your health and perfect weight are those that provide calories without nourishment, such as fast foods and other highly processed foods like packaged cookies, doughnuts, and soft drinks. Each day, you are creating your trust in your ability to choose the foods that work *for* your health and perfect weight, not *against* your health and perfect weight. By being mindful of your internal cues for hunger and fullness, you discover what is intuitively "right" for you, and that lets you give these foods your trust. You must also be able to trust the food you are eating to deliver the nutrients that satisfy you body's needs and your hunger. By staying loyal to your relationship with food, you not only develop the ability to choose the foods that

---

MOTIVATION MAKER

Hunger Can Be a Good Thing

Ever so many years ago, hunger was a signal from nature that told us to start hunting and gathering food. Way back then, it took a bit of time to get a meal ready. So people really worked up an appetite. These days are a lot different. We get a little twinge of hunger and it takes just a few moments to quell the feeling with a snack. We rarely know what real hunger feels like. However, the important fact here is that *hunger helps us enjoy our food much more.* The next time you feel a little hungry and it is not time to eat, remind yourself that you will savor your next regular meal much more if you first work up a good appetite. We don't encourage not eating when you are hungry; we do encourage allowing your body to use the food you've fed it and enjoy foods when it is hungry.

---

deliver what you need with pleasure but you also develop a palate that appreciates these nourishing foods. These pleasurable foods are fresh, vital, and brimming with health and nutrients and great taste. If your food is not delicious and pleasurable, choose again. Over time, you discover that you can trust the relationship you have created to sustain the lifestyle and eating style that lets you *eat whatever you want and keep your perfect weight.*

Breaking Up Is (Not) Hard to Do!

Dump the foods that have empty calories and don't nourish you. There may be things you eat out of habit, such as cake or white-flour dinner rolls; break up with them. Say goodbye to foods that make you feel guilty. Stay loyal and committed to the foods you love that are also healthy for your body and your perfect weight.

Write a "Dear John" or "Dear Joan" letter in your journal. List the foods that you want to break up with (perhaps pizza or beer or cheese puffs or doughnuts), and write down why you want to break up with them. Do they make you feel guilty? Do they betray your perfect weight by providing only empty calories? Do they just provide brief respite from emotional turmoil when you are mad or sad? Or do you eat them when you are bored?

Write a "love" letter in your journal. List the foods that you have a love affair with (such as fresh fruits and vegetables and brown rice) and write down all the attributes of those foods that are so attractive and lovable. Do they make you feel energized and strong? Do they make you happy? Do they satisfy your real hunger? Do they support your perfect weight?

It Is All About Loving: Spice It Up

Your love affair with food and eating is all about loving: loving what you are doing and loving yourself doing it. Project your feelings of love into this magnificent makeover you are giving yourself. Include your food, too; love it. Let yourself get passionate about the food and eating that create the results you want.

Every relationship needs some spice sometimes. What is your favorite spice? Pick up some recipes for Mexican, Thai, East Indian, Moroccan, or Mediterranean dishes and start experimenting with flavorful spices. The spices will help you enjoy the palate changes that are taking place in your makeover and weight loss. Spices also help you feel better in other ways. For example, use turmeric or ginger to reduce tissue inflammation, capsaicin in chili peppers to release endorphins, and garlic to boost your immune system.

On a trip to Santa Fe, we bought a book about cooking with chili peppers, and now we make our own very tasty

---

IN THEIR OWN WORDS ...

I was initially skeptical that self-hypnosis could make a difference in my ingrained eating and food-buying habits. But early on, I began to see a difference in how I ate, and what I was looking forward to eating. These already noticeable changes accelerated when I started doing daytime and nighttime trancework CDs, to the point where now, just a few weeks later, I look forward to indulging in lovely, fresh vegetables. Previously stress would have sent me straight to a chocolate bar and/or the liquor cabinet. The Gurgeviches are absolutely right when they say that all you have to do is listen—your unconscious mind will do the rest. I highly recommend this program to people who are thinking twice about their eating habits, weight, and general health. You owe it to yourself to discover the joys of pushing your plate away halfway through a meal because you're happily satisfied.

SARAH

and spicy Chili Colorado (red chili sauce) that gets us up and dancing. Spices also bring new life and new possibilities to foods you might be bored with. Unprocessed foods like vegetables and lean protein can taste a million different ways depending on which spices you pair with them. Spices liven up your love affair with food. Experiment with them to spice up your eating experience.

Make It Sensual

Every romantic relationship has an element of loving sensuality. Choose to make your relationship with food and eating a sensual experience. Begin with your cooking. Immerse yourself in the sensory experience of preparing food. As you wash and rinse your food, smell the earthiness of the fruits and vegetables, pay attention to what the food feels like in your hands, and imagine that your fingertips touching that melon or lettuce leaf are as sensitive as if you were caressing something you love. Run your fingertips over the curves of the vegetables; feel the outer surfaces; feel the inner surfaces after cutting them open. Hold the food to your nose and really notice the subtle aroma of your food. Remember, if you do not love this relationship, how can you expect it to endure or be rewarding to you?

Color, Texture, Aroma, Taste, Chew

Train yourself to put more attention on the sensory pleasure of eating a meal. Before you sit down to a meal, write these words on five separate cards: color, texture, aroma, taste, chew.

Sit down and serve yourself the portions of food that you want on your plate. When your plate is ready, place the cards next to your plate. Close your eyes and sit calmly for one or two minutes with the meal before you. Because your visual sense is the most stimulating, by closing your eyes, you are immediately slowing your body down. These moments with your eyes closed give you time to focus on your sense of smell.

Make a game of noticing the different foods you placed on your plate. Focus on the aroma of the foods and any spices. Perhaps you may wish to use this time to quietly recite an affirmation about the nourishment of your food and the perfect body weight you are fueling.

NOURISHING AFFIRMATIONS

- My food provides excellent nourishment for my perfect weight.
- My food satisfies my hunger.
- My food gives me the energy I need to enjoy my active lifestyle.
- My food gives me all the nutrients I need to be healthy and happy.

Open your eyes and begin eating your meal. Stay tuned to the sensory richness of this meal. The card with the word "color" is a reminder to notice and appreciate the colors on your plate. See if you can taste each color or smell it. The card that says "texture" is your reminder to feel the texture of each food with your mouth and tongue. Is the texture crunchy, smooth, soft, slippery, or hard? Notice the aroma as you hold the food on your fork or spoon near your nose before putting it in your mouth. Really *smell* the food to increase your sensual pleasure of eating. "Taste" is the reminder to notice the flavor of what you put in your mouth. Is it tangy, salty, sweet, sour, bitter, spicy? Notice other aspects of your food: is it hot, or cold, or tingly? Move the food around in your mouth with your tongue. Allow all the taste buds to experience the food's flavor. Lastly, "chew" the food slowly and pay attention to chewing as an act of relishing each mouthful. Think of "chewing" as part of loving your food. Allow yourself to feel the love and pleasure of your dining experience as you focus attention on the physical experience.

The more pleasurable your sensory experience, the more control you have over noticing colors, tastes, textures, aromas, and noticing when you are getting full. As you swallow each bite of food, pay attention to the sensations in your stomach. As you get full, your stomach will have a very comfortable feeling, and you will have less sensory pleasure with each extra bite. That is good, for that lets you be aware of when you have eaten enough—when you should push your plate away.

Tools of the Trade

Treat yourself to the kitchen tools that will make food preparation stimulating and pleasurable for you. (If you like waffles, buy a waffle iron. If you like smoothies, buy a blender.) Shop in the kitchenware department of your favorite store and in kitchen boutique stores. Find the tools and utensils that nourish your love affair with food and eating. This goes for your dining experience as well. Choose plates and dishes that will make you want to set a lovely table for yourself, complete with place mats, glasses, and candles. Make mealtime a cherished ritual. Think of it as a ritual that leaves stress behind and brings you a sense of calm, peace, and satisfaction. This is a love affair, remember? The investment in your recipe for a loving relationship with food and eating is worth every penny.

Perhaps delving into the kitchen is too big a leap for you right now. If so, become a connoisseur of ethnic restaurants and other eating establishments that prepare wholesome foods. Keep a folder of restaurant addresses and menus. Become the "person in the know" regarding great places to dine. But please remember, many nourishing and delicious foods need no preparation at all. Sitting down to breakfast at home with a plate of bananas

Dieting is not the answer to keeping weight down. As you have heard many times, almost all people who diet to lose weight regain it (and more). Instead, you need to change long-term patterns of eating and physical activity. Hunger management is key. New patterns of eating must satisfy both physical hunger and the need for sensory pleasure from food.
ANDREW WEIL, M.D.,
Eating Well for Optimum Health

and strawberries and a piece of bread with cashew butter is the epitome of simplicity and requires zero preparation other than the swirl of a knife.

MOTIVATION MAKER

Become a "Gearhead"

"Gearheads" are people who love their hobby and interest so much that they fall in love with all the accoutrements or special gear involved with that interest. If it were not for gearheads, specialty and boutique hobby shops would not exist. In the kitchenware department, the gearheads are the ones who ask about the latest in peeling-utensil grip materials, serving-ware temperature ratings, and power ratings for food processors.

Develop a New Vocabulary

Did you ever notice how new lovers and newlyweds speak to each other? They often have their own vocabulary that they only share with each other. For many, it seems to enhance their experience. So why not pay some attention to your vocabulary in your relationship with food? You do not have to invent cute little terms of endearment for your vegetables, but we would bet that you may still use terms like "fattening," "lite," "low-fat," "hi-calorie," or "dieting." *These words have to leave your vocabulary.* Build a vocabulary of words that reflect the pleasure in your relationship with food. Use words like "sumptuous," "tantalizing," "creamy," "elegant," "luscious," "satisfying," and "nourishing."

Take a moment to write down in your journal a list of words that make you feel good when you hear them. These include the words you use to describe any aspect of eating. When you hear someone say, "I'll just grab something on the way to work" in reference to a meal, consider that language. If you were feeling romantic, would you dream of settling for just *grabbing* something? Pay attention to the words you use, and create the vocabulary that enriches your pleasure in food and eating. The mind of your body will notice the difference before you do.

The multibillion-dollar diet industry uses buzzwords to create demand for its products. "Low-cal," "low-fat," "no-carb," and "sugar-free" are just a few. Take notice of how these words affect your feelings about your food and eating. If "lite" meals are your thing, fine. But if they are only reminders of self-deprivation, ask yourself, "What can I substitute that lets me feel good about my meal and myself?" The "real thing" comes to our mind, and we do not mean that popular sugary beverage. Rather, the real thing (food that is very close to nature and unprocessed) in appropriate quantities, prepared in a way that tantalizes your taste buds and is a feast for your eyes and tummy, will work much better than trying to appease yourself with some disguised so-called lite or diet food.

> Bread is the warmest, kindest of words. Write it always with a capital letter, like your own name.
> On a Russian café sign

HERE ARE SOME EXAMPLES OF REPLACING DIET-BASED FOODS WITH UNPROCESSED, WHOLE FOODS

- Serve real butter rather than lite margarine.
- Serve whole-grain crackers rather than no-carb cookies.
- Serve pure apple juice rather than sugar-free soda.
- Serve real maple syrup rather than low-cal pancake syrup.
- Make chicken and vegetables rather than a frozen "low-cal" meal.

Robin Kanarek, professor of psychology and nutrition at Tufts University, tells us that when people eat foods designated as lite or low-fat, they compensate by eating other foods with even more calories. Her findings are consistent with studies on drinking sugar-free diet drinks. The research on diet soda shows that individuals who drink it do not lose weight, but may actually overcompensate by thinking they can consume other foods. The message: Do not fall prey to the delusion that lite, low-cal, low-fat, sugar-free foods allow you to eat sweets and treats. Instead, choose the "real" foods that nourish and satisfy you and your love affair with food, and which result in your perfect weight.

BELIEF BOOSTER

Toss the Scale

Throw away the bathroom scale, and get your finger off the pulse of how many pounds you weigh. Focus on your health. The scale can't tell you how healthy you are, how fit you are, or how good you feel.

Communication and the Art of Listening

Anyone who has consulted a marriage counselor, read a book about relationships, or seen a talk show discussing relationships knows this word: communication. You have to be able to communicate with your partner. It also works in your relationship with food. Communication and patterns of interactions that enrich and sustain a relationship are important.

Food has the ability to communicate. It is always talking to you. The real art of communication is in listening. You "listen" with your taste buds, the tactile nerves in your mouth, your nose, your eyes, even your ears. And you "hear" the results produced in your body, such as how energetic, happy, full, and satisfied your food makes you. When you eat without listening, you might overeat. *If you listen when you eat, you will know when you are full, and you will stop eating when you are satisfied.*

Stress and a New Normal

If you do not love your relationship with your food and eating, it is doomed to failure. It is normal to experience stress in any relationship, and as you make changes and adjustments to your food and eating, you will notice what has not yet become familiar. There will be the stress of adding and subtracting ingredients to your recipe for your love affair with food. But this should only be stressful until the patterns of habit or familiarity are established. Later we will speak about "small tastes," those gradual slow changes that you will choose as you become more comfortable and familiar with your new lifestyle. Through repetition, you will create patterns that become familiar to your mind and body and, in essence, a "new normal" is established that works much better than what you replaced. The more mental techniques you use to de-stress the experience of change, the easier and faster you create what becomes "normal" to you.

The New Norm

Norm came to our clinic, determined to lower his cholesterol without taking the medications his doctor was suggesting. Norm was originally from Wisconsin and grew up eating all the delicious local dairy products. His childhood tastes remained with him as an adult, and he had a habit of drinking two to three glasses of whole milk every day. We advised that he make the switch to 1 percent milk. He balked at this advice, but he finally agreed to do it for "just two weeks." Two weeks later, this is what he said: "I just couldn't think of drinking 1 percent, so I bought 2 percent instead. For the first few days, I really noticed a difference between the 2 percent and my whole milk. But I really love milk, so I just drank it. After a while, the 2 percent actually tasted pretty decent, especially right before bedtime with an oatmeal cookie dunked in it.

When the 2 percent carton was empty, I bought the 1 percent just like you asked me to, and I couldn't really tell the difference between the two. But this is the clincher: Yesterday, I went over to my buddy's house and grabbed a carton of whole milk out of his fridge. I can't believe it, but it tasted like thick cream. It really didn't appeal to me at all."

Norm's taste buds and palate easily made a transition, and established a new normal that works much better for him now. By the way, after one month of drinking 1 percent, and switching from ice cream to frozen yogurt, Norm's cholesterol dropped forty points!

Easy Does It

Jerry was sitting in a recliner in our office for a session of hypnosis. During the trancework, he abruptly sat up, opened his eyes and asked, "Can't you just tell my subconscious that I swallowed a pill that makes me feel full?" He was frustrated and just wanted a simple and easy solution. After some thought, we proceeded with the trancework. I spoke to him about going deeply into trance, wherein he could imagine a journey into a forest. I encouraged his imagination to follow the trail until he reached an area where the ground was covered with beautiful ferns. He moved the fern leaves aside, and on the forest floor he found mushrooms that glowed. Not all the mushrooms glowed, only those that were safe to eat. I instructed him to gather fourteen of the glowing mushrooms in a basket, and after leaving the forest, he was to place them in a glass jar. I gave him the post-hypnotic suggestion that whenever he wanted to eat before a meal something that would let him enjoy the feeling of fullness, he could go into trance and open the jar and eat just one of the mushrooms. His subconscious had his permission to use the mushroom to help him feel full for one meal. After the trancework, we talked about his trance experience, and I encouraged him to practice his hypnosis after arriving home from work, just before he prepared and ate his meal.

When we saw him again, he was delighted to tell us how well he was doing with his hypnosis. He described practicing his hypnosis very regularly before his evening meal and popping one imaginative glowing mushroom into his mouth during his trancework. That one "mushroom" produced a wonderful feeling of fullness such that he would prepare and eat a light meal for his dinner. He made it successful because it was what he wanted. He allowed himself to believe in what he wanted and expected for himself.

When you nourish your love affair with food, you will love eating and you will do it well, and you will discover the joy of food. Your love affair with food will allow you to recognize your real hunger and satiety, and it will seem as if you can eat anything you want and still keep your perfect weight.

CHAPTER 8

CLEARING THE PATH TO YOUR PERFECT WEIGHT

*Obstacles don't have to stop you. If you run into a wall,
don't turn around and give up. Figure out how to climb it,
go through it, or work around it.*

MICHAEL JORDAN

The path to your perfect weight will probably be fraught with pitfalls, land mines, and saboteurs. Any worthy goal has obstacles to be overcome. This chapter is about recognizing those obstacles, dismissing some of them, and taking bold action to eliminate the others. The hypnotic trancework focuses on thoughts and ideas at the mind-body level which will energize the process. Familiarize yourself with thoughts, old patterns of behavior, special social events, and everyday settings that might potentially sabotage your perfect weight. This is the first step toward clearing the path to your perfect weight. Once you are able to recognize the triggers to overeating, you simply need to practice ways to easily dismiss those seemingly troublesome obstacles. If this seems overwhelming, don't worry. As we've said, we will guide you in your trancework so you may communicate exactly what you want to say to your magnificent mind-body.

Where Are You Right Now?

As you begin your path, assess where you are now. New numbers from the United States Government's National Health and Nutrition Examination Survey (NHANES) confirm that overweight and obesity are still a major public health concern. According to data from 1999 to 2002, 65.1 percent of adults aged twenty or older were overweight or obese. The rate of obesity was 30.4 percent, and 4.9 percent of U.S. adults were extremely obese. Overweight is defined as having a body mass index (BMI) of 25 or higher. Obesity is having a BMI of 30 or higher. Having a BMI of 40 or higher is extreme obesity.

To determine your BMI: Divide your weight (in pounds) by the square of your height (in inches) and then multiply that number by 703. Keep in mind that a person who is muscular with a low body-fat percentage may have a higher BMI because muscle weighs more than fat.

So, if you are 5'8" and weigh 185 pounds, your BMI is 28. To see where you are right now, compared with other Americans, look at these statistics:

Nearly two-thirds of U.S. adults are overweight (BMI of 25 or higher, which includes those who are obese).

Nearly one-third of U.S. adults are obese (BMI of 30 or higher).

Less than half of U.S. adults have a healthy weight (BMI higher than or equal to 18.5 and lower than 25).

Getting Out of Your Way

Safeguarding your success and clearing the path begin with you. As you read in the earlier chapters, everything begins with thoughts and beliefs about what you want, how you want it, and what you can believe and accept. All self-defeating thoughts must be neutralized and transformed into affirmations of your success. For example, if you continually say, "My belly is the biggest part of my problem," what are you telling your mind-body? What is your mind-body going to make true for you? Here is the affirmation that neutralizes and transforms that statement and other statements like it: "My body is perfectly shaped." When you encounter thoughts that don't support your perfect weight, remember this affirmation and follow these four steps.

> Stand up to your obstacles and do something about them. You will find that they haven't half the strength you think they have.
>
> NORMAN VINCENT PEALE

1. You must believe it is possible for you to have the perfect weight you desire.
2. You must want it and feel you deserve it.
3. Accept any challenge as an opportunity to have your perfect weight.
4. Let yourself expect the results you desire, and commit yourself to removing any obstacle from within or without.

IN THEIR OWN WORDS ...

Thank You! I find my food cravings are greatly diminished and my food choices are nutritious. I was a stress eater. Now when I feel the uncontrollable urge to eat overtake me, I take a deep breath, press my index finger and thumb together, hold, then release. It is a miracle to be able to regain immediate control before I have time to "impulse eat." What a wonderful feeling of success to have control of my eating! I am a tough critic, but I am a complete believer in the healing power of this program.

GEORGENE

NOURISHING AFFIRMATION

Every day in every way,
I am getting slimmer and slimmer.

Letting Go of Old Patterns of Behavior

Patterns of behavior with food, eating, and exercise must become increasingly compatible with the results you want. Here are some ways to start shifting your perspective:

- If you love junk food, you must let go of a *daily* diet of junk food and welcome some new, healthier foods that support your healthy weight.
- If you have an aversion to exercise and physical activity, you must welcome the daily physical activity that enlivens and strengthens your body.

The same is true for the subconsciously driven patterns that create cravings. You start by identifying incompatible cravings as obstacles and mark them for removal. This tells your subconscious that it has your permission to act on your behalf. The trancework contains suggestions that empower you to welcome new patterns of behavior.

MOTIVATION MAKER

Bad Food

If you order something in a restaurant and it turns out to be mediocre, leave it on the plate, even though you paid for it. Eating food that doesn't satisfy you only creates a desire to eat more of something else. Even though you have "wasted" you money, that is better than eating something you are not enjoying.

Excuse You

Clear away all excuses you give to yourself and others. They only work against you. Here are a few excuses we hear from our clients:

"I don't have time to do any shopping and cooking."

"My job is too stressful, I couldn't possibly add more stress by dieting."

"When the kids are out of the house, then I'll have time to think about losing weight."

"I can't lose weight. My knees hurt too much."

Make a sign for your refrigerator: "Exercise ONLY on the Days That You Eat."
JAMES ROUSE

MOTIVATION MAKER

We need to stop focusing on what we are doing wrong, and focus on what we have stopped doing right. Think back to your childhood, your carefree play, your delight in popping fresh-picked blueberries in your mouth. Learn to move as you did when you were a child, with joyful, natural, and effortless motion.

Here are some ways you can start moving now:

- Make dates for physical activity (power walks, playing sports).
- Walk homeless animals at the local animal shelter.
- Consider virtual fitness, such as streaming a yoga instruction video. A study published in the *Psychology of Women Quarterly* revealed that women who practice yoga are happier with their appearance than women who practice regular aerobic exercises.

There is *no* excuse that justifies an obstacle to your success. This includes any excuse about the expenses associated with weight loss. Yes, quality foods may cost more than fast food, but your perfect weight is worth every penny and every pound lighter. We have had patients tell us that weight loss programs are too expensive or that their health insurance will not cover the expenses of a weight loss program. No amount of money is a valid excuse to keep you from achieving success. The medical conditions associated with excess weight will cost you more in the long run. If your investment in the problem *outweighs* your investment in the solution, you will keep the problem.

Do not make excuses because you feel you lack willpower. If you have the willpower to breathe clean air or read this book, you have the willpower necessary for everything else you want in your life. Become sensitive to the excuses you hear others using, the reasons that they say they cannot have what they want. Pay particular attention to individuals who are overweight as they speak about the obstacles to their weight loss. Some other excuses we've heard are: "I don't have the time or the energy to make breakfast in the morning," or "It's sprinkling out, I can't take my fifteen minute walk tonight," or "The holidays start next month, I'll wait until January." Each time you hear an excuse, make a mental note for yourself: "Not for me" or "I know better." In the television series *In Living Color,* Damon Wayans played a reluctant clown named Homey, who would go to birthday parties to entertain children. When the kids would ask him to do the slapstick and self-deprecating activities that clowns are famous for, he would decline, saying, "Homey don't play that." However funny this was, he actually had a point. He was dressed as a clown, but he never sacrificed his self-respect or integrity for anyone, even when it was his job. When you hear yourself or others make any excuse that might affect your perfect weight, tell yourself with a smile, "I don't play that" and "I have a better way."

Judge Righteously

Obsessions about food or weight can be obstacles to successful healthy weight. To break these patterns, take bold action to defuse, neutralize, or transform any obsessive thoughts, such as

> ## MOTIVATION MAKER
> ### *Change Your Habits*
> Watch a movie while clenching tennis balls with your hands or knitting instead of eating ice cream.
>
> Read the Sunday paper while giving your feet a bubbly soak or riding your elliptical workout machine instead of sipping on a calorie-laden latte.
>
> Enjoy the companionship of your hungry teenager or spouse while they eat, by sipping a cup of hot tea or a glass of sparkling water if you aren't hungry instead of having your fourth meal of the day.
>
> Remember, there are alternatives. You always have a choice. You do have the willpower to change your habits.

Obstacles are things a person sees when he takes his eyes off his goal.

E. JOSEPH COSSMAN

"I'm always hungry," "All I think about is food," or "I have to eat." This may mean talking to a counselor if it is an obsession that warrants clinical intervention. If you feel that you cannot change obsessive thoughts by yourself, you will probably benefit from professional help.

If it is *not* a serious psychological obsession, begin examining your judgmental thoughts. That is, if you are giving food and/or weight too much of your mental energy and thoughts, you can change the judgments and thoughts that you are making. Since your goal is to achieve your perfect weight, you want to cancel the thoughts that let food control *you* and transform those thoughts so that *you* control the food. Either your obsessive thoughts about food will drive you, or you will drive them. Choose to judge with the "right" thoughts, the thoughts about food that will be a path to your perfect weight. A few examples: "My breakfast was delicious," or "The pita pocket I packed is full of pep and power," or "I love the grapes I had for dessert." In short, if you are going to obsess about food, make it work for you by obsessing about your success. Make your judgments righteous: make them correct for you.

Metabolic Obstacles

It only makes sense to rule out any underlying organic or metabolic obstacle to your perfect weight. The first one that comes to mind is thyroid function. In her book *The Thyroid Diet: Manage Your Metabolism for Lasting Weight Loss,* Mary Shomon notes that almost thirty million Americans have a thyroid condition, and half of them go undiagnosed. To see if you qualify, your physician can run comprehensive testing to determine whether you have any thyroid or other metabolic dysfunction.

If you are unable to exercise due to illness, accident, or disability, you can do isometrics. This is the simple technique of tensing muscles against an object or even another body part and holding for about twenty seconds. Press your hands together at chest level for arm and upper body strengthening, and push your feet against the floor to strengthen the thigh muscles. *The Complete Book of Isometrics* by Erin O'Driscoll is an excellent resource.

Another common metabolic obstacle is the weight-gain effects associated with antidepressant medication therapy. Antidepressants come in three major categories: tricyclics (e.g., amytriptyline, also known as Elavil), selective serotonin reuptake inhibitors (SSRIs such as Paxil and Zoloft) and monoamine oxidase inhibitors (MAOIs, much less frequently used). Each can affect appetite, carbohydrate cravings, and metabolic changes that increase weight. If you are using an antidepressant, you may want to talk with your physician about using the lowest *effective* dosage, since it is usually the higher dosages that cause the greatest problem with weight gain.

Narcotics are another class of drugs that can influence weight gain. Narcotic analgesics (pain relievers) have two factors that may affect weight. First, all opiate derivatives or narcotics have a depressing effect on the central nervous system, which causes the natural peristalsis, or wave-like motion through the digestive system, to slow down, which in turn may slow other aspects of metabolism. Second, individuals with pain usually have mobility problems that limit their physical activity. For some, the CNS (central nervous system) depressant effects may limit physical activity even further. Some of the non-narcotic medications may have alternatives, but as with antidepressant use noted earlier, the *effective* dose and drug is the first priority.

MOTIVATION MAKER
Sleep Deprived?
When you are tired, do you crave food? Studies indicate that adequate sleep (eight to nine hours per night) may aid in controlling levels of hormones involved in appetite. *Get more sleep.* It is difficult to cope with everyday stresses when sleep is inadequate. And it is difficult to refuse that convenient piece of cake when your body is tired and craving a quick pick-me-up. (See chapter 9 for more about sleep.)

Disabilities and Handicaps

Anyone who has experienced an injury that limits physical activity knows how quickly weight can increase. Individuals with disabilities or handicaps that limit or preclude physical activity and exercise have to be creative in this regard. A consuming mental challenge can sometimes affect weight loss. Although we have no empirical research to substantiate the relationship between expending mental energy and weight loss, we do think it is worth considering. For example, taking a class which requires intense mental energy may actually consume calories and also serve as an alternative to eating inappropriately. Another idea might be to consult with a physical or occupational therapist and explore inventive ways to strengthen those parts of the body than can be actively moved. Isometrics are often an excellent option (see chapter 9).

You Control the Inertia

Inertia is the force that keeps a body at rest or in uniform motion. In order to move an object that is at rest, there must be a sufficient force to overcome the energy that is keeping the object at rest. You may have become comfortable with the amount of inactivity you experience, and this level of inactivity is the *inertia* that maintains your current activity level. Increasing your physical activity level requires enough force or energy to overcome the inertia. You can think of a ball that is at rest and the energy required to "get the ball rolling." We recommend using stimulating rewards to overcome the inertia and propel you into physical action. Let it be simple. Climb the stairs instead of riding the elevator, and reward yourself with a cold, crisp apple. Or create a *bigger* reward. Set up a travel savings account as a reward for attending a workout center. If the rewards do not overcome the inertia, they simply are not rewarding enough yet. The bottom line is that you control the forces that overcome the inertia.

Invigorating Activity

... in the same way you will improve physical fitness by developing good, sensible habits of exercise that you can stick with for the rest of your life.
ANDREW WEIL, M.D., *Natural Health, Natural Medicine*

Young children don't join fitness centers or walk purposefully around the block after dinner to lose weight. Watch them. They move whenever there is opportunity. When they could sit, they stand; when they could stand, they walk; when they could walk, they run or climb or jump or do cartwheels. In the same way, we all benefit from spontaneous physical activity, whether climbing the stairs when we could take the elevator, parking at the far end of the parking lot when we could park near the door, walking to the corner drugstore when we could drive the car, or briskly walking several blocks to catch the bus one stop farther down the street. A fifteen-minute phone call could be fifteen minutes on the elliptical machine. As busy as we are, our daily lives present myriad opportunities to be physically active. Our pursuit of daily fitness does not have to be conducted in one large session, but rather we can do it in spurts throughout the day, with the same benefits. It all adds up, and our bodies love to be nourished with activity as well as wholesome food. Not only do we nourish ourselves physically through movement, but we nourish ourselves emotionally because regular physical activity is calming to the mind.

You might ask: "What is the best exercise for me to do?" We say, "Whatever you will enjoy and whatever you will do for the rest of your life."

Procrastination

Procrastination is the intentional and habitual postponement of doing things that you say you want to do. It is definitely a form of self-sabotage. Procrastination is the *choice* to *not* do what will move you to your goal of perfect weight. There are many strategies for dealing with procrastination.

If you are procrastinating about changing from a sedentary to an active lifestyle, start by walking around the neighborhood for fifteen minutes every day, rather than committing to a seemingly daunting one-hour, five-times-a-week fitness center schedule. Start small, and take on more as you feel comfortable and ready. Do it in a way that suits you. Perhaps you have a personality that would rather commit to diving right in without taking time to think yourself out of it. Or it might be helpful to find a partner who will stimulate you to do it until you unlearn the old behavior. We like the Nike slogan: "Just do it."

Educate Yourself

Remember, your weight is not the result of the mistakes you have made; it is only the unwanted result of how you have been living. A recent Yankelovich Preventative Healthcare Study surveyed six thousand adult Americans regarding issues of health. It found that close to 65 percent of Americans have never attended a nutrition class and 50 percent have never taken a fitness class. Since 65 percent of Americans are overweight, could there be a correlation between being overweight and the absence of information about nutrition and fitness? We think so.

Jonathan came into our office, oblivious to why he might have gained twenty extra pounds. He related to us that several years earlier he had fallen in love with a young entrepreneur who bought a franchise of a nationwide ice creamery. Jonathan began indulging in nightly treats brought back from the new store. It didn't take long for those treats to take a toll on his physique. Once he made the connection between the extra calories and the extra weight, he cut back on the nightly treats and began riding his bicycle every day, which burned off the extra weight.

Leap, and the net will appear.
JULIA CAMERON,
The Artist's Way

> ## MOTIVATION MAKER
> *Stand When You Can*
> Slim people stand about 150 minutes more each day than obese people. Just that simple change burns 350 calories. Stand while talking on the phone. Stand while waiting for the dentist appointment. Stand while waiting for a friend.

How does this translate? What you do *not* know can make you overweight. The advertising budget for fast-food companies far surpasses the education budget for nutrition. We have assembled a just-what-you-need-to-know collection of facts in chapter 9. The trancework on your CD includes hypnotic suggestions for your mind-body to effortlessly act upon everything you read and hear about wise lifestyle choices.

Getting Others Out of Your Way

Now let's look at the obstacles in your path that others present. These obstacles include the obvious and hidden saboteurs in your daily life with family and friends, at office gatherings, at special social events and holidays, while traveling and dining out, when being a target for weight discrimination, and in your own kitchen. These obstacles primarily involve others, but still require some action and attention on your part to protect your perfect weight. You just need to become more familiar with the possibilities for sabotage, and practice how to best handle anything or anyone that "attacks you from behind." The good news is that you ultimately are responsible for your choices in all these situations. The trancework on the CD will offer suggestions that tell your subconscious mind-body ways to handle possible sabotage.

BELIEF BOOSTER
Let Your Body Do the Math
Don't bother counting calories. Determine your food intake by how you feel in your clothes, how much energy and vigor you have for your daily activities, and how you look in the mirror.

With our clients we have seen that often the greatest form of sabotage will be come from those closest to you, your family and friends. If you have been on a diet in the past, you already know about diet saboteurs. Perhaps they mean well, perhaps not. Change is not easy for everyone, and when you announce that you have made changes to your eating routine, others may not understand what that means for them or what changes this may impose upon them. They will simply fall back on the familiar routines with you that they have known in the past. When others seem to sabotage your efforts you must determine why they are behaving contrary to your goals. If it is simply *the change,* then perhaps they mean well but just do not yet understand what to do to support you. A few well-spoken words that explain kindly and clearly your new intentions will do wonders here. "I know I *used* to always have a double scoop of strawberry ice cream after dinner, but *now* I only eat when

Anything can be achieved in small, deliberate steps. But there are times you need the courage to take a great leap; you can't cross a chasm in two small jumps.
DAVID LLOYD GEORGE

Procrastination is, hands down, our favorite form of self-sabotage.
ALYCE CORNYN-SELBY

I'm hungry … so, maybe later I'll have a scoop." Or, "Actually, I brought over a great new treat: strawberry sorbet."

MOTIVATION MAKER

If you taxed one penny for every soft drink sold in this country, you'd raise $40 billion a year.

KELLY BROWNELL, behavioral psychologist at the Yale Center for
Eating and Weight Disorders, *Eating Well,* May 2005

There may be other factors that influence the sabotaging behavior of family and friends. It is not uncommon for those around you to feel guilty when you are doing something to achieve your perfect weight and they are not. Your success is a reminder to them of what they should be doing for themselves. Face it: with over 65 percent of Americans being overweight, you will only encounter three out of every ten individuals who will *not* have a reason to feel guilty around you. So what can you expect from those that feel guilty around you? Food! They will give you food to bring you back to where *they* will feel comfortable.

Phrases that "protect" you in this scenario are:

- "I only eat when I'm hungry."
- "I'm watching what I eat right now."
- "It looks/smells delicious. Could I have the recipe?"
- "I would love to have some later, when I am hungry."
- "I'm not eating sweets these days … but I'd love to have some of those grapes over there."
- "My allergies seem better when I avoid …. " (By the way, we notice that there seems to be a blind respect for allergies. People accept allergies as a very "legitimate" excuse to refuse food.)
- "For some reason I have more energy when I avoid …"
- "My body feels ill when I eat … I think I'll pass this time."

Your friends and family may sabotage your efforts as an attempt to re-establish normal and customary interactions with you. Perhaps they miss those special brownies that you always brought, or the huge portions of lasagna that you shared before *you changed*. They simply miss the you they knew how to interact with over food. They did not change. You did, and the changes that involve food now affect them, too.

Fear

A very common reason for sabotage that we hear in our clinical practice is *fear*. Your partner's security about your relationship together can be a great source of fear. The idea that makes your partner fearful is that you will become more attractive and leave them for someone more desirable, or someone else will now find you more desirable and try to take you away. We can honestly say that this issue of security with a partner comes up in almost 100 percent of the partnered individuals we know who are successful in achieving weight loss. One case that stands out was observed at the Johns Hopkins Health and Weight Clinic over twenty years ago. A twenty-seven-year-old woman came to receive help in reducing her weight from 300 pounds down to a healthier 145 pounds. An evening session was scheduled for the patients to bring their spouses with them to the clinic. During the session, the woman's husband admitted that he would bring home a frozen cream pie each night from work and *make* her eat it. She had never mentioned a word about his abusive behavior, but he broke down in tears and spoke of how frightened he was of losing her if she were to lose weight. This case may seem exaggerated, but it does reflect a dimension of fear that we see in almost all the individuals we work with at our clinic. Sometimes it is an offhand remark like "If you lose weight, you won't leave me for someone else, will you?" Even the slightest remark of that kind shouts, "I am afraid."

Forms of diet sabotage may include insults reflected in remarks like "Isn't my food good enough for you anymore?" or "What's wrong with eating supersize fries? You always used to like them." Perhaps people feel distanced from you or think that you do not like them anymore and that is why you eat less, or "pass" on certain dishes, or don't come over for dinner or go out to lunch as often as before. You will have to determine for yourself what motivates their sabotaging behaviors. The important concept is to not allow it to sabotage your path to success. There are eating rituals that will always continue to a certain extent, and that's okay. The sharing of foods and desserts will always happen because food is a strong social connection. Most bonding activities and traditions involve a table or platter of food. But now you can politely defuse those land mines with a simple statement such as "Thank you, but I am carefully choosing what I eat right now. It looks delicious, but I *want* to pass on it today."

MOTIVATION MAKER

Lunchtime Tips

Many people have lunchtime and workplace behaviors that do not support their perfect weight. Here are several tips:

- Ban fast food. Just refuse it. There are so many healthy and truly delicious alternatives.
- At the office, stash healthy food in both the fridge and the freezer to avoid circumstantial or situational food choices. Ninety-six percent of American lunches are from fast-food restaurants.
- Eat a healthy and substantial lunch *before* running lunchtime errands. Running errands first puts you at risk for skipping a meal or grabbing a quick calorie-laden filler.

In ancient Greece, it was one of the basic duties of a good citizen to be responsible for his health so as not to be a burden on society.

Salubrity is a state of well-being that extends beyond physical health to also include healing, hospitality, and personal responsibility. Health is living in an integrated state of mind, body, and spirit. Healing is the continuing integration of new experiences of the mind, body, and spirit. Hospitality is the kind and accepting manner in which we treat each other. As for personal responsibility—there is no other way than to consciously be responsible for ourselves.

MOTIVATION MAKER

Have a light, wholesome, and mindful meal (a bowl of soup, a salad, some whole-grain bread) before joining a party or other food-laden occasion. Then you can concentrate on socializing. Mindless eating is rampant at social gatherings. But don't deny yourself. Choose *one* food that you know you will enjoy, perhaps homemade bread or a special dessert, and enjoy. That's it. That's all.

Occasions to Eat

The path to your perfect weight will be strewn with birthday parties, bridal and baby showers, award banquets, christenings, bar mitzvahs, weddings, graduations, and many other celebrations. On any given day, it is always someone's birthday. It may seem as if you are constantly dealing with the eating pitfalls associated with special occasions that involve food.

If you are mentally prepared—consciously and subconsciously—you will do fine. Think of these occasions as you would a tournament you are going to play in: practice and rehearse your performance as you wish it to be. Your mental rehearsal with your self-hypnosis will surprise you.

At the completion of a special project at work, treat yourself to a yoga or exercise class at your neighborhood fitness center.

When you notice your jeans are loose (and this *is* cause to celebrate), go out and buy two new pairs that fit your new body fantastically.

Curl up in bed with a stack of magazines or a great book.

Light some candles and play your favorite music CDs and dance, as though no one is watching.

SALUBRITY (n.) (from the Latin *salubritas*) Wholesomeness; healthfulness; favorableness to the preservation of health; as the salubrity of air, of a country, or a climate.

Webster's New World Dictionary of the American Language

"Stuffing-More-Than-the-Turkey" Days

We had one patient refer to the holiday season between Thanksgiving and the New Year as "my next six pounds." Thanksgiving is famous as a time to eat wonderfully delicious food beyond the point of no return. The challenge with the "holiday season" is that it can be unrelenting with food, stress, and joy—but mostly food. First, remind yourself that you are not alone. As a society, how did we ever let these holidays become so consuming, of food and otherwise? Perhaps a better question is "How do we *not* consume more than what benefits our perfect weight during these joyful times?" The answer is in preparation and substitution. Your self-hypnosis rehearsal will prepare you to deal with the meals, your appetite, and stress.

You can find ways to substitute sensibly delicious foods for the unhealthy calories. Here are some examples:

HOLIDAY "FAVORITES"	SENSIBLY DELICIOUS SUBSTITUTES
Standing Rib Roast	Roast Turkey
Yams with Marshmallows	Baked Yams
Sausage Stuffing	Cornbread Stuffing with Apples

APARIGRAHA
The yogic term for
greedlessness;
the importance of
not taking more
than we need or
can use. Practice
aparigraha.

HOLIDAY "FAVORITES"	SENSIBLY DELICIOUS SUBSTITUTES
Green Bean Casserole	Roasted Vegetables with Olive Oil
Cranberry Jelly	Whole Cranberry Sauce
Waldorf Salad	Fresh Grapes, Apples, Bananas
Pumpkin Pie	Pumpkin Pie, just one piece (What's Thanksgiving without pumpkin pie?)
Ice Cream	Frozen Yogurt or Sorbet

In holiday situations, use your self-hypnosis to mentally rehearse the outcome that will serve you and your perfect weight. Maintaining your weight throughout the entire holidays is admirable; losing weight during this time is downright holy. Before the holidays, choose the results you want and how you want to feel. Visualize your success when you practice your self-hypnosis.

Kitchen Land Mines

In chapter 7, we spoke of the necessity of selecting an environment (and foods in that environment) that is compatible with your perfect weight. Clearing out the land mines that could blow up your progress is another step in clearing the path to your success. Chapter 9 will guide you through the steps to purging your pantry and defusing the explosives. We would like to mention here that your success is at risk if you keep anything in the house that can undermine the results you want. If it is not in the kitchen or refrigerator, it cannot tempt you or hurt you. It is not a matter of deprivation, going without, or giving up the foods you like. This is about you creating a lifestyle that you enjoy every day and that also provides the perfect weight you want.

The safest "convenience foods" to have in your pantry for when you are "starving" or "can't wait to eat" and are tempted by "roadside calorie traps" are:

- canned peaches, pears, or apricots (without sugary syrup)
- canned tuna or salmon or sardines
- canned chili with beans
- frozen entrees such as enchiladas and burritos or other health-oriented meals (no TV dinners, please)
- frozen hamburger patties or vegetarian patties, and frozen wholegrain buns (it only takes a few minutes to fry a frozen patty, so put it in the pan while you go change your clothes)

Remember, these pantry items must be delicious enough to lure you home without going to a "drive-thru," but you also want them to be several levels healthier than the typical fast-food choices. You are protecting your healthy weight by *not* succumbing to the fast-food industry that has established an outpost on every city street corner.

MOTIVATION MAKER
Restaurant Tactics

Speak up and ask questions at restaurants. Ask for what you want (steamed vegetables instead of fried rice, dressing on the side, hold the mayo).

Be the *first* to order (in a crowd) to avoid the copycat syndrome. "He's having a sub and a beer. I'll have one, too."

The Safest Take-Out

Traveling can pose some challenges until your lifestyle is on autopilot. Many feel that being away from home minimizes their choices or confounds their routine. It is more challenging, but it can be done. The best solution is to take some food with you. Pack a meal or snacks that will last until you arrive at your destination. Airports always offer fast food, but today there are a few healthier

- Normal eating is going to the table hungry and eating until you are satisfied.
- Normal eating is being able to choose food you like and eat it and truly get enough of it—not just stop eating because you think you should.
- Normal eating is being able to give some thought to your food selection so that you get nutritious food, but not being so wary and restrictive that you miss out on enjoyable food.
- Normal eating is sometimes giving yourself permission to eat because you are happy, sad, or bored, or just because it feels good.
- Normal eating is three meals a day—or four or five—or it can be choosing to munch along the way.
- Normal eating is leaving some cookies on the plate because you know you can have some again tomorrow, or eating more now because they taste so wonderful.
- Normal eating is overeating at times, feeling stuffed and uncomfortable. And it can be undereating at times and wishing you had more.
- Normal eating is trusting your body to make up for your mistakes in eating.
- Normal eating takes up some of your time and attention but keeps its place as only one important area of your life.

In short, normal eating is flexible. It varies in response to your hunger, your schedule, your proximity to food, and your feelings.

ELLYN SATTER, *Secrets of Feeding a Healthy Family*

options in airport food courts. The Physicians Committee for Responsible Medicine, a preventive-medicine advocacy group based in Washington, DC, conducted a survey of fifteen of America's busiest airports. It found a 7 percent increase in wholesome food choices. We don't think this is a very impressive statistic, but it does indicate movement in the right direction. You may find choices ranging from Cuban restaurants, sushi bars, and salad bars to eateries that serve grilled vegetable sandwiches, portobello mushroom sandwiches, and roasted vegetables panini, to mention a few. Trains are a delight for dining; some are akin to cruise ships. They usually have menus that let you satisfy your hunger and keep your perfect weight. Traveling by car allows you to drive right to a grocery store to get exactly what you want if you cannot find a healthy restaurant. Whole Foods, Wild Oats, Trader Joe's, and other health-minded grocery stores even have healthful prepared meals for purchase.

SOME OF OUR "TRAVEL COMPANIONS"

- walking shoes and visor
- bottled water
- tea bag assortment
- dark chocolate (at least 60 percent cocoa)
- dried fruit
- whole-grain crackers and cookies
- nuts and seeds
- turkey jerky
- the old "standby": a fresh apple
- homemade granola or a plastic bag of our favorite store-bought granola

> If the industrial food giants provided only nutritious, healthy foods, the diet and health-care industries would be very different.

Buying into Stealthy Advertising

When you see food advertised on television, in magazines, on billboards, on the radio, in theatres, even in hospitals, remind yourself that this can also be a form of sabotage. Perhaps the only aspect of advertising that is sabotaging for *you* is that which seduces you into believing that you are hungry for the product and want a colossal serving. But another major deception used in food advertising is painting a healthy picture of unhealthy ingredients, such as hydrogenated oils, animal growth hormones, cottonseed oil, high-fructose corn syrup, chemical coloring and flavoring, excitotoxins, preservatives, carrageenan, the many pesticide, herbicide, and fungicide residues that have systemically grown into the food itself—and the list goes on. Advertising is tested and based on research that has demonstrated the greatest response rate. It is very unlikely that the local farmers' market will be enticing you on television to buy locally grown fresh fruits and garden-grown vegetables. The advertising you see will usually be for food that is laden with sweeteners, unhealthy fats, and artificial colors and flavors, and it will have popular and appealing images that make you want to buy the product. Make yourself conscious of what the ad might really be pushing. Yes, it may taste good or make you feel good while you're eating it, but it is fleeting satisfaction. A patient once described his first experience with heroin: "It is as if every desire you've had in your life came to the surface of your mind and was satisfied a hundred times greater than you could imagine." The bottom line is this: see the sabotage for what it is; do not buy into being fooled to risk your perfect weight.

MOTIVATION MAKER

How to Sidetrack a Craving

- **Assess the Situation**

  Are you hungry? Or are you uncomfortable?

  - Would you rather indulge right now, or stay on track with your goal of perfect weight?
  - Is this food wholesome and nourishing to your body, or might it sabotage your goal of perfect weight?

- **Remind Yourself**

  Eat only when hungry. Stop when full.

  - I will have a healthful treat later.
  - My goal is important to me.

- **Indulge Yourself**

  Converse with an interesting person.

  - Breathe deeply, in and out, five times.
  - Vividly imagine your perfect body.
  - Promise yourself a wholesome treat soon.
  - Smile and keep talking/walking/listening.

"The Devil Made Me Do It"

Flip Wilson portrayed a character named Geraldine on *The Flip Wilson Show,* who would rationalize her actions by saying, "The Devil made me do it." If you are overweight, you may find yourself feeling defeated or hurt when others discriminate or make judgments about your weight. Many of our patients tell us that when they are the object of discrimination or bias, they want to eat to comfort themselves, or simply give up and fulfill their defeat with food. The path to your perfect weight will include some devils that may tempt you to throw your efforts aside and just eat something to make yourself feel better. Unfortunately, you know that this form of relief is very short-lived, and the resulting guilt is often worse than the original offense. Here again, being prepared and rehearsed with your self-hypnosis defuses the emotional charge of this obstacle. Stay true to your goals and you will not let the insensitivity of others sidetrack you.

Angry John and Angry Blisters

John was carrying about eighty extra pounds when we first met him. When people made comments about his weight or judged him, his hurt feelings would quickly turn to anger. He came to our clinic because of the anger, not his weight. He was very good at suppressing his anger, and when it started coming out as angry blisters with a case of shingles (herpes zoster), his physician sent him to learn self-hypnosis for stress relief. A large part of his problem was his job. He is a parish priest, and his job prevented him from displaying anger toward others, even when they deserved it. He was not a very good hypnotic subject at first but, as happens with most people, he got much better with practice. During the trancework, I offered hypnotic suggestions that he would find a productive channel for his anger. One of the nice things about hypnosis is that you do not have to be specific in telling your subconscious how to do its work. You can be very specific at times, with rich imagery, but there are other times when you just ask for what you want and let the subconscious come up with something creative on its own. In John's case, he was very well-disciplined in practicing his self-hypnosis each day. Within two weeks, his shingles were healing very rapidly and effectively. By the end of the month, his shingles were gone—and so were fifteen of those extra pounds. He had not intended to lose weight, and we did not mention his weight in the trancework. What John discovered was that each time he got frustrated, which is a form of anger, he would drop what he was doing and go walk a lap or two around the park across the street from the church. John told us that he never really thought about exercise or walking, but after he started self-hypnosis, it just seemed to happen for him. He created a walking meditation that allowed him to redirect any anger into blessings. Later that year, we saw him at the farmers' market and commented about the fifty pounds he had shed. He told us that the weight loss was the blessing in the meditation for him.

MOTIVATION MAKER

Boost Your Metabolism

Your body burns about fifty calories a day to maintain each pound of muscle. It burns about two calories a day to maintain each pound of fat. Move faster. Get a calendar and write down each day how long you have walked. Gloat about it.

Plateaus

Geographically, a plateau is a large land mass with a starkly level surface that extends far above the surrounding land. A plateau is an impressive landmark, and when one stands atop it, the view is spectacular.

Figuratively, a plateau is an unchanging or stable situation, time, or condition. Distance runners become ecstatic when they reach a "plateau" during a long run, for that brings them to a time when their gait is smooth, their breathing is regular, and they are "on a roll." It is a time when they can assess how much distance they have covered on the run, and how to pace themselves for the remainder of the course. They are neither pushing ahead nor lagging behind. They are steady and strong. They have "hit their stride." They are "doing it."

We invite you to embrace your weight loss plateau with the same invigorating attitude. You've come a long way to reach a plateau. Take a look at the spectacular view. Perhaps you have initiated changes in physical activity or in healthier food choices. Perhaps you have cleared aside a few obstacles on your path. Perhaps you have broken down an emotional barrier. And for certain, you have lost weight.

Ponder your success and tap into what Eckhart Tolle calls "the power of now." The "now" moment is very different from where you were "then," when you first began to use self-hypnosis and make changes. The "now" moment allows you to see with great clarity what you have accomplished up to this point. But more importantly, the "now" moment allows you to see with even greater clarity the *remaining* steps to your perfect weight. On this plateau, for example, you may easily see the path toward more time for self-care, such as a longer evening walk. Perhaps you will realize you actually want to get more serious about hiking, so you join a hiking club. Or maybe, up until now, you begrudgingly wrote your journaling exercises, but now you see writing as quite inspirational, and you set aside *more* time for writing. The view from high atop the plateau allows you to see new directions to your perfect weight that might have seemed unimaginable to you when you first began your weight loss efforts. Now it's time to take a deep breath, focus, and move ahead.

The Five Impossible Tasks

Sandra was exasperated that her weight loss had come to a stand-still. She was truly stumped to come up with a way to move off her plateau. We gave her an assignment: "Use your hypnosis to go back in time. Imagine yourself at the time *before* you began your weight loss efforts that brought you to the plateau. Make a list of the five most unimaginable accomplishments that would affect your weight loss."

When she returned, she was glowing with self-satisfaction. Her mood and spirits were up, and her weight was going down even further. She told us that when she was writing down the five unimaginable things to achieve weight loss at that time, it dawned on her just how far she had already come. What seemed unimaginable back then seemed like great ideas now. She signed up for a weight-training class, started jogging three times a week, organized herself to do her grocery shopping every Thursday evening, and decluttered her garage. But the most amazing "task" to Sandra was that she stopped drinking wine. Before the plateau, she had always told us, "I could *never* give up my wine. I love it too much." Sandra realized that when she felt stuck on the plateau, she was still in the mindset of when she first began, and was not in the "now moment." As soon as she readjusted her "view," she was able to see what she could actually do now, so she could move herself ahead.

Brush and floss your teeth more often. Brushing is a sign that people care about their health. It cleanses the mouth and clears the palate, and may be that extra incentive against snacking.

Write It Down

As you walk along the path to your perfect weight, write down realistic goals in your journal. There is magic to writing things down, and a magic to the spoken word, too. Use these goals to formulate your own ideas and affirmations of what you want for your perfect weight. Keep your affirmations hidden from saboteurs, and pull them out each day to review them. Speak your affirmations out loud so that your ears bring the message in from the outside as well as bring what you absorb from within you. Tweak and adjust them so that, ultimately, you are absolutely clear about what you want. As you use the self-hypnosis on the accompanying CD regularly each day, you will find that after a month or so, you will be infusing your own ideas, images, and suggestion into your trancework.

It's a Date

Start scheduling social activity with friends and family away from the dining table or restaurant. Make dates to go for a walk or meet outdoors or in places where you might enjoy a cup of tea and a conversation. Keep the goal for your perfect weight a priority so that it happens. Make a date with every flight of stairs, and take a vow to forego the elevator or escalator. Park so that no one will dent your car doors. That is, park as far away as you safely can, so that you walk the distance.

Shhh—Keep It Secret

If you knew the exact time and place to purchase the next winning national lottery ticket, you would not broadcast the information. In the 1963 movie *It's a Mad, Mad, Mad, Mad World,* before Smiler Grogan (Jimmy Durante) literally kicks the bucket when his car careens over an embankment, he tells onlookers he's stashed $350,000 in stolen loot beneath "the big W" in the town of Santa Rosita. Thus begins a mad dash to recover the dough. "The big W" for you is your perfect weight. Keep it to yourself. Only tell those who are partnering with you to help you achieve your goal.

CHAPTER 9

TAKING CARE OF YOU— EXPLORING WHOLESOME FOODS AND OTHER WISE CHOICES

I don't eat junk foods and I don't think junk thoughts.
PEACE PILGRIM

We have all watched young children and how they absorb their world: eyes wide open, touching, tasting, smelling, listening, all with delight, total impulse, *and* energy and motion. We invite you to approach this chapter with the same childlike curiosity. Allow your mind to explore every idea, fact, and suggestion, for this chapter is filled with sensible information on which you can base your lifestyle choices. You may pick and choose what appeals to you and your perfect weight, what nourishes your physical hunger, and what inspires and invigorates you.

Hungry for Wholesome Foods— Sensible "Eativity"

Our bodies are composed of billions of cells, and these cells are the basis of every function of the body: eyesight, fertility, breathing, brain functions, immunity, skin rejuvenation, movement, and digestion, among the thousands and thousands of functions. The food we eat is the only sustenance available to our bodies to create and replace these cells. The vitality of every one of those cells is dependent upon the quality of food that we eat. If we eat foods that are wholesome and nourishing, the cells will be strong and vital. If we eat nutrient-poor foods, junk foods, highly processed foods, foods high in salt, sugar, and bad fats, or highly refined foods, the cells will be weak and will struggle to perform their functions. Highly processed foods (which are nutrient-poor) are often very high in calories. A poorly nourished body craves nourishment, and if that craving just leads to more junk food, then there are far too many calories consumed with no nutrient satisfaction. Poor health and excess weight may follow. It can be an endless cycle until it is broken with wholesome foods. That is why 65 percent of Americans are overweight. Their undernourished bodies are overfed with poor food choices. When we nourish our bodies with wholesome foods, we feel better, have more vitality, and are more physically active; and healthy weight is the result.

> You cannot get down to your ideal weight and stay there by making resolutions to diet, going on the latest fad diet, joining a diet center, or buying pills and drinks that promise magical results. You can do it only by changing your ways of eating permanently, by building up good, sensible food habits that you can stick with for the rest of your life.
> ANDREW WEIL, M.D.,
> *Natural Health,*
> *Natural Medicine*

MOTIVATION MAKER
Pursue Your "Health" Hobby

Buy a few books or subscribe to a magazine or newsletter that helps you find and cook nourishing foods. (See Further Reading and Resources for more information.)

Everything we eat should contribute to our health and be absolutely delicious. Our clients hear us say this all the time. Everything we eat should contribute to our health and be absolutely delicious. It can be a little confusing to decipher exactly which foods *are* wholesome and contribute to our health. There is one simple statement to hold in mind that will clarify all the perplexing nutrition input screaming at us from TVs, magazines, books, and grocery store shelves. *The most wholesome foods, the foods that nourish our bodies the best, are closest to nature.* These foods are fresh, alive with vibrant colors, aromas, and flavors. They are minimally processed; they are not canned, not frozen, not preserved, not artificially flavored, not colored with coloring agents, not hydrogenated, not genetically engineered, not sprayed with pesticides, not raised with agrichemicals, not heat treated, not homogenized. *They are closest to nature.* Now, you might be thinking that there isn't much left to eat after reading that. Maybe you just took a mental walk through your kitchen. Maybe you are frowning and standing in front of your favorite crackers, cookies, cake mixes, frozen TV dinners, ice cream, hot dogs, and pizza. The point is that there are so many highly processed foods available that it is often a challenge to even *find* the wholesome foods. But you need to find them. You want to be hungry for wholesome foods because they support your excellent health and perfect weight.

IN THEIR OWN WORDS ...

I have been working on the Self-Hypnosis Diet for eleven days now and have lost eight pounds. I am not exercising much (yet) other than parking farther away in parking lots, and am not on any special diet plan other than eating whole, healthy foods, limiting dessert to one time per week, and making sure I eat at least three times a day. I have found it amazingly easy to make healthy food choices, and I credit self-hypnosis.

SALLY

It Starts with a Few Small Tastes

Take another mental walk through your kitchen again. Do you see any fresh fruits, fresh vegetables, brown rice, beans, almonds, or sunflower seeds? If so, you already have some nourishing foods in your pantry. All we are inviting you to do is take a few small tastes, to consider making a few simple shifts toward sensible food habits.

MOTIVATION MAKER

Morgan Spurlock's *Super Size Me* is a "must see" movie if your food choices, or those of someone near and dear to you, include fast food. The average American eats three burgers and four orders of fries each week. Half of our nation's family food budgets are spent in restaurants, mainly at fast-food chains. How are we fueling our children? Are we supporting their healthy weight?

We would like to introduce you to the Behavioral Nutrition Continuum. It is a very useful tool for you to use in making shifts in food and lifestyle choices. The first step is finding your starting place on the nutrition continuum. On the extreme left of this continuum are those whose diets consist mostly of high-calorie, nutrient-poor foods: high in fat, salt, and sugar; highly processed; and non-organic. They are the product of the fast-food movement, and they also are not mindful of the environment surrounding food—the who, what, when, where, why, and how. Moving toward the right end of the continuum, we find those whose diets consist mostly of whole foods, such as grains, beans, and fresh fruits and vegetables, and fewer animal foods. These foods are nutrient-dense, fresh, and alive with vibrant colors, aromas, and flavors, and are close to nature. Do you know where you are on this continuum? Where are your family and friends on this continuum? When you see people who have bodies like the one you want, chances are they are closer to the right end of the continuum.

Just be aware of your spot on the continuum right now. It doesn't matter where you are. What *is* important is the direction you are moving toward. It will change with time as you use just your own awareness and begin with a few small and simple shifts. Over the years, we have discovered that it is of utmost importance to move at your own comfortable pace. This allows your taste buds and palate plenty of time to shed the intensely salty, sweet, fatty flavors that have dominated your plate for perhaps many years, and to begin savoring the refreshing flavors of nourishing foods. So start where you are on the Behavioral Nutrition Continuum. And start with a few small tastes of wholesome foods that lead you in the direction you want to go.

How to Know What You Are *Really* Eating

Another useful tool is learning to decipher the Nutrition Facts and Ingredients labels that are on all packaged, canned, and frozen foods. Both labels are important but for different reasons. The Nutrition Facts label defines *quantity,* and the Ingredients label defines *quality*. Walk into your kitchen and select a Nutrition Facts label from any packaged product. The label contains information regarding the approximate amounts of various nutrients in the specified food. As you will see, serving size and servings per container are stated first. The number of calories per serving and calories from fat are listed next. The section immediately following lists in grams the total fat, saturated fat, cholesterol, total carbohydrate, dietary fibers, sugar, sodium, and protein contained in each serving. The micronutrients, the vitamins and minerals, are listed next. In addition, the percent daily value (a set of standard nutrient intake values developed by the FDA) is calculated on the label, and is based on a 2,000-calorie diet. What this means is that if you're eating 2,000 calories a day, the percent daily value stated next to a nutrient listed on the product tells you what percentage of your daily needs for that nutrient are being met by that product. You should develop the habit of reading all food labels in your kitchen and at the grocery store.

> ### MOTIVATION MAKER
> Read nutrition labels when you are shopping. It is difficult to eat an unhealthy food when you read for yourself how unhealthy it really is. There is a very empowering sense of responsibility when you choose to eat with integrity and be informed about nutrition. Discover the healthy alternatives—they are often close by on the same shelf.

When examining labels, make certain you relate the number of calories to the serving size. Often the stated serving size is very small, with a corresponding low-calorie advertisement. For example, a candy bar may advertise only 50 calories per serving but the serving size is only a small part of it, not the entire bar. Now, if you have them in your kitchen (if not, look the next time you are in the supermarket), select the Nutrition Facts labels of two similar products such as crackers or cookies. Compare the categories of total fat, saturated fat, cholesterol, and sugar. Notice that when a product advertises that it is low-fat, it is often high in sugar. And when it advertises low-sugar, it is often high in fat.

Now look at the Ingredients label, which lists the actual contents of a product. By the way, to read this label, you might have to put on glasses. The Ingredients label is notorious for being impossible to read, thanks to minute print, lack of contrast between letters and background, or being printed on the fold of the wrapping. The Nutrition Facts label may state that the total fat is 4 percent, but the Ingredients label will specify *which* fat or oil the food contains—olive oil, cottonseed oil, partially hydrogenated sunflower oil, etc. Another example in which the Ingredients label clarifies quality involves carbohydrate content. If the Nutrition Facts label lists total carbohydrates as 42 grams, one can glance at the Ingredients label and see whether the carbohydrate is derived from white flour or a more health-promoting grain such as bulgur, brown rice, or amaranth. The Ingredients label also alerts the consumer about food additives and animal products, many of which are of concern. A food additive is a substance added to food during its processing to preserve it or alter its color, texture, flavor, or value. Flavoring agents make up the largest single class of additives and include salts, spices, essential oils, and natural and synthetic flavors. Additives that alter texture include emulsifiers such as lecithin, stabilizers, and thickeners such as guar gum, xanthum gum, and carrageenan. The additives used to preserve food are primarily chemical microbial agents such as benzoates, propionates, and sorbates. Antioxidants are added to food to prevent fats and oils from becoming rancid and to prevent discoloration of smoked or canned meats. Antioxidants such as tocopherols, vitamin E, retinoids, vitamin A, ascorbic acid, and vitamin C help retard spoilage. There is controversy concerning the safety of some additives, so educate yourself. A good reference book for food additives is *A Consumer's Dictionary of Food Additives* by Ruth Winter, M.S.

I'm easily satisfied with the very best.
WINSTON CHURCHILL

A GOOD RULE OF THUMB
If the Ingredients label is more than one line, the product might have some unhealthy ingredients. So read the list carefully.

Pantry Purging: Taboo Foods

Keep in mind that the food you want in your pantry (and ultimately on your plate) is the highest quality that you can afford. High quality means: fresh, whole, locally grown if possible, homemade, nutrient-dense, organic (grown without the use of conventional agrichemicals such as pesticides, growth hormones, prophylactic antibiotics, etc.), and appetizing with *real* flavor (not masked with chemical flavors and artificial colors).

Take an honest look in your pantry and refrigerator. Start reading a few of the Ingredients labels. Now is the time to get rid of the foods that do not belong there, that you *know* do not promote your health and perfect weight. When you "purge your pantry" you make room for the nourishing, fresh foods that you will be buying on your next grocery shopping trip.

Take a cardboard box into your kitchen. You will be filling it with foods you no longer want to eat. At the end of this exercise, you will take the cardboard box out of your home. Throw it in a Dumpster or give it away.

Consider putting in a cardboard box foods containing refined white sugar, high-fructose corn syrup or corn syrup of any type, glucose, and artificial sweeteners. The average American consumes two pounds of sugar weekly. This is not only in the form of refined white sugar, so just throwing away the sugar bowl isn't going to work. White sugar has many disguises, such as brown sugar, which is usually just refined sugar sprayed lightly with molasses to give it a healthy look, and turbinado sugar, which is only one refining step away from white sugar—again, with just a healthier look but negligible nutrition. Corn syrups, such as high-fructose corn syrup and the light and dark corn syrups, are another refined sugar in disguise. They are chemically purified corn starch, hydrochloric or sulfuric acid, and water. Corn syrup is in soft drinks and candy, bakery items of all sorts, fruit juices, bottled spaghetti sauces, and ketchup, to name just a few. The average American consumes seventy-nine pounds of corn sweeteners every year. *Do not eat them.* They oppose your healthy weight. Read the Ingredients labels in your pantry closely.

Consider putting in a cardboard box foods made with white flour, such as doughnuts and pastries, and conventionally produced crackers, cookies, breads, and muffins. White flour and products made with white flour are devoid of nutrients, as those nutrients have been eliminated during the processing of the grain. You are about to begin tasting a variety of grains: kasha, barley, brown rice, quinoa, amaranth, spelt, rye, kamut, oats, etc. Many ready-to-eat breakfast cereals contain these grains, and there are many bakeries that bake breads with these grains. Whole grains and legumes are the only food which contain all the macro nutrients. They are nutritional powerhouses. They have protein, carbohydrate, good oil, B vitamins, vitamin E, and fiber.

MOTIVATION MAKER

If we could eliminate one item from the American diet, it would be chemical sweeteners, such as Sweet 'n Low, Equal, and NutraSweet, that are used in diet sodas and sugar-free candies and gums. Chemical sweeteners are a "no-no" for our bodies. Don't be fooled by diet sodas and other sugar-free foods. They only give false hope. A study from the University of Texas Health Science Center at San Antonio revealed that people who drink one diet soda every day have a 55 percent chance of becoming overweight. This is 22 percent more than regular soda drinkers. It seems that diet soda drinkers often indulge in extra calories elsewhere. Do yourself a favor and stop drinking diet sodas right now.

Consider putting food containing poor-quality fats in a cardboard box. This includes hydrogenated oil, partially hydrogenated oil, margarines, cottonseed oil, and products containing them, such as microwave popcorn, most conventional crackers and cookies, cakes, pastries, potato chips, leftover fast food, etc. You will replace these inferior products with delicious and satisfying foods made with healthful oils. Once your eye learns to spot these unhealthy oils on the package's ingredient label, you will quickly discover the nearby healthy alternatives.

Consider putting non-organic dairy and meats in a cardboard box. All conventionally raised dairy and meats in America are full of harmful agrichemicals. Of special interest are the growth hormones given to animals to promote weight gain (and thus more profit at the marketplace). If your goal is to lose weight, we do not recommend eating animal products that contain traces of growth hormones such as BGH. If you choose to eat animal products, choose grass-fed beef, free-range poultry and eggs, and organically raised and produced meats. In addition, you should eat a minimum of dairy and limit that consumption to organically produced milk, cheese, yogurt, cottage cheese, and butter. Dairy products signal trouble for many people. You may be one of them. The fat in dairy is saturated, so if used in excess it can create heart health problems. (Many of us look for low-fat milk but we neglect to recognize the fat in ice cream.) One of the proteins in dairy, casein, is an allergy trigger for many people. Lactose, the carbohydrate or sugar in dairy, frequently causes uncomfortable gastrointestinal symptoms because many people lack the digestive enzyme lactase. Be mindful of your dairy consumption and listen to your body's reactions.

Consider putting foods containing caffeine in a cardboard box. Coffee, black teas, sodas, and chocolate are all high in caffeine, which causes great fluctuation in blood sugar levels. In turn, this can lead to anxiety, sleep disorders, hypertension, and myriad other symptoms. These foods should be used very judiciously, if at all. A good *dark* chocolate, containing at least 60 percent cocoa, is an exception. Dark chocolate contains flavonols, antioxidants that help our bodies fend off free radicals, some of which are naturally generated in our bodies, but are also created when we eat unhealthy hydrogenated and partially hydrogenated fats found in highly processed foods. Flavonols also help boost the healthy HDL cholesterol and lower the not-so-healthy LDL cholesterol levels in our bodies.

Most probably, there are some *very* favorite foods in the pantry that you are discovering are taboo and, if you live with other people, there are probably foods in your pantry and fridge that are someone else's favorites. Everyone near and dear to you needs to eat more wholesome foods, not just you.

BELIEF BOOSTER

Increase plant-protein foods and decrease animal protein in your diet. Research shows that a low-fat, whole-food diet that is mostly vegetarian is health promotion at its finest, whereas the standard high-fat, high-protein American diet is dangerous to your health. In addition, from a global perspective, if Americans reduced their meat intake by 10 percent, sixty million people could be fed adequately with the grain that would be saved. So the bottom line here is to use meat as a condiment or a side dish rather than an entrée. When we say meat, we mean beef, pork, and chicken. You don't need to eat a steak that is so big it laps over both sides of the plate.

SMART DESSERT
Ounce for ounce, dark chocolate has five times as many antioxidants as blueberries. Dark chocolate is a good choice for an occasional dessert.

Make gradual changes (remember, small, simple "tastes" at the beginning) for some of these favorites.

- Buy frozen yogurt to replace the ice cream.
- Slowly replace chips and cookies with nuts and whole-grain crackers and cookies.
- Buy frozen cherries and pineapple pieces to replace artificially flavored popsicles.
- Buy whole-grain frozen waffles to replace cinnamon rolls made with white flour.
- Buy organic turkey hot dogs to replace high-fat, nitrated, all-beef hot dogs.
- Buy one of the excellent herbal coffee substitutes, and have one cup of regular coffee and one cup of an herbal drink. A latte is delicious when made with one of these botanicals. Or simply buy a decaffeinated coffee, as a first small "taste."

Choosing wholesome foods always gives the body an opportunity to function optimally. If you don't pump the highest grade fuel into your Ferrari, the engine will start to knock and you won't get the highest performance. It's the same with our bodies. We often take better care of our vehicles than our human bodies. It doesn't make sense. We can go out and buy a new car, but we can't buy a new body.

Pantry Staples: What to Put on Your Shopping List

We should eat about 60 percent of our daily calories in high-quality carbohydrates (grains, fruits, and vegetables), about 20-25 percent in high-quality fats and oils, and about 15-20 percent in high-quality protein (plant proteins like nuts, seeds, and beans, or lean meats, or a combination of these). These combinations of nourishing foods are the perfect sustenance to create those billions of strong and vital cells that are your body.

> **BELIEF BOOSTER**
>
> The average American eats only fifteen different foods. This usually means orange juice, coffee, doughnuts, bagels, iceberg lettuce, tomatoes, carrots, hamburgers, fries, pizza, hot dogs, cheese, pasta, ice cream, and soda. From that list, how much is fresh and alive with vibrant colors and aromas and flavors and goodness? What kind of fuel does it provide?

The next step to filling your kitchen with wholesome foods is to make a shopping list. Following are suggestions that we feel are central to a healthy kitchen pantry and refrigerator. You may already have some products in your kitchen. Make a note of the items you feel you would like to incorporate into your cooking.

- A bottle of Italian or Greek olive oil, a bottle of canola oil, and if you wish, a small block of organic butter (used sparingly) and a small bottle of sesame oil
- Nuts (almonds, cashews, walnuts), nut butters such as cashew butter or almond butter
- Seeds (sunflower and pumpkin) and legumes (anything in a pod, so all beans, including edamame—soybeans) are high in plant protein and healthy oils.
- Choose a grain for the week. We would suggest quinoa. It is light and delicious, and cooks in fifteen minutes. But you can choose from a variety of whole grains (brown rice, oatmeal, kamut, spelt, buckwheat, wild rice, etc.).
- Find a ready-to-eat cereal that contains a variety of grains (oatmeal, buckwheat, brown rice, kamut, etc.).
- Bread and pastas made with whole grains
- Frozen whole-grain breakfast waffles
- Crackers and cookies made with whole grains and healthful oils
- Potatoes and sweet potatoes
- Onions and garlic
- If you wish to eat dairy, 2 percent milk and plain yogurt (organic)
- If you wish, lean animal protein (organic chicken and turkey are best, organic turkey or chicken hot dogs).
- An omega-3 essential fatty acid source, such as flax seed, walnuts, or pumpkin seeds
- Fish is an especially healthy choice for protein if it is from cold waters. Wild salmon, mackerel, sardines, and herring are all very high in omega-3 essential fatty acids also.
- A can or two of beans (such as pinto, black, navy, or kidney beans)
- A can or two of tomatoes and pasta sauce
- Five or more different colors of fresh vegetables (beets, tomatoes, squash, kale, spinach, carrots, purple cabbage, etc.)

- Five or more different colors of fresh fruits (cherries, bananas, blueberries, green apples, cantaloupes, kumquats, plums, etc.)
- A few herbs and spices like oregano, basil, dill, curry, and cinnamon
- A bottle of tamari sauce or soy sauce
- Browse through the tea aisle. Rooibos tea is a very flavorful caffeine-free herbal tea, which can be served hot or iced. Green tea is very healthful, but it does contain caffeine, although less than coffee and black tea. Those are our favorites, but there are many from which to choose.
- If sodas are still a "necessity" for you, as an alternative buy some sparkling water and frozen concentrated fruit juice. (Mix a spoonful or two of frozen concentrate—grape is delicious—with iced sparkling water for a delicious, healthful zing.)
- If coffee is your thing, experiment with one of the botanical coffee substitutes. Remember, taste buds need gradual changes to adapt to new tastes, so just experiment with a cup and gradually increase as you are enjoying it. Coffee is one of the most heavily pesticide-sprayed crops in the world, so if you do buy coffee, buy organic and fair-trade.
- Experiment with healthy sweeteners such as brown rice syrup, stevia, or maple syrup. Rapadura is very unprocessed sugar cane and is an excellent "first taste" when cutting down on white sugar. If this is too big a "first taste," just begin to cut down on the amount of white sugar you use.
- A few bags of frozen fruit pieces (pineapple, mango, cherry)
- Frozen yogurt to replace high-fat ice cream or other rich frozen desserts
- Lastly, we always have a supply of good dark chocolate for dessert (60 percent cocoa or more).

Finding Wholesome Foods: Where to Shop and How to Shop

Most conventional grocery stores now have sections where you can find healthier food options. They are usually called "organic," "health," or "whole" foods sections. You have to look and ask. There are also entire stores devoted to healthier choices. Many health-oriented food stores have displays and opportunities to sample foods. "Food tasting" is very enticing and is a fun way to experiment with new flavors and textures.

A good rule of thumb when you walk into your grocery store is to shop the periphery of the store. That means push your cart around the outer edges of the store, which is where the bakery, fresh produce section, coolers with juices and yogurts, meats, and fresh fish counters are positioned. We rarely go to the center of the store (except for frozen fruits and vegetables, and canned beans) because that is where many of the more highly processed foods are stacked. No refrigeration is necessary for these highly processed products and their shelf-life is long. Many contain preservatives, additives, agrichemicals, sugar, salt, white flour, and hydrogenated and other unhealthy fats and oils.

BELIEF BOOSTER

We can't say it enough: Eat when you are hungry. Stop eating when you are full. We tend to overeat and consume too many calories when we have been undereating (skipping meals, eating a low-calorie diet). In addition, when people adhere to low-calorie diets, those diets do not supply enough calories to adequately fuel the body, nor is the vitamin and mineral intake sufficient to maintain health. Also, when the body senses that it is not getting enough fuel, it slows all the bodily functions down to keep the body alive. This slowing down of the metabolism means fewer calories burned, which defeats the purpose of weight loss. The bottom line? Skipping meals or following an extreme low-calorie diet ultimately means taking in too many calories by splurging or overeating, health problems, and slower weight loss.

As you approach the fresh produce aisles, stop and feast your eyes. Just enjoy for a moment the enticing rainbow of colors, *all from nature*. On your shopping list we suggested five colors of fruits and five colors of vegetables: raspberries, cherries, beets, squash, pineapple, peppers, blueberries, purple potatoes, broccoli, kale, red peppers, kumquats, tangerines, sweet potatoes, purple cabbage, purple onions, and grapes. Use a rainbow of colors and we guarantee that you will be never be bored with your food. In fact, it will be the greatest gift to your taste buds and your body, and you can never eat too many fresh fruits and vegetables. They *always* support your perfect weight.

A very pleasant alternative to grocery stores is your local farmers' market. Fresh air, pleasant conversation with farmers, and freshly picked, locally grown produce turn grocery shopping into an outdoor venture.

HEALTHY MUNCHIES

One cup of popped popcorn has two grams of protein. Drizzle it with a bit of olive oil and a dash of sea salt as it comes out of the hot-air popper.

From Pantry to Plate

It's one thing to have all the good foods in the kitchen; it's another thing to know how to put them together to make an easy, quick, delicious meal. If you are new to the kitchen, learn how to steam, how to do a stir-fry, and how to bake. Take a beginner's cooking class at a community education center, find a cooking show on cable TV, or browse through a few instructional cookbooks at your local bookstore some afternoon. If you are new to cooking and your cooking tools are limited, here are some basics you should have:

- a wok or a frying pan (cast-iron pans are inexpensive and indestructible)
- a 1-quart or 2-quart pot with lid
- a stainless steel steaming basket that fits inside your pot with a lid
- an oven-proof baking dish
- four nesting bowls
- a good knife, spatula, and a few wooden spoons
- a cutting board
- a blender
- a hot-air popcorn popper

MOTIVATION MAKER

How to Snub Excessive Snacking

Keep snacks in sealable containers. You are less likely to grab a handful if you have to pry off a lid. When you walk into the kitchen, have something in one hand (mug of tea, bottle of water) so that you can't easily grab a snack. Finally, if you must have a snack, eat any fruit or any vegetable. Pack a handful of nuts or dried fruit in single-portion plastic bags, and stash them in the desk drawer.

The Supersizing of America

America is the land of supersize portions. American restaurants serve huge portions and expect us to eat those portions in twenty minutes. When that big helping is in front of us, we tend to ignore our natural sense of fullness. We have become so accustomed to these portion sizes that we have even increased the portion sizes in our own home cooking. Next time you are having pasta at home, dish out your portion onto the plate. Measure that portion, and you may be surprised. A standard serving of pasta or rice, according to the Nutrition Facts label, is one-half cup. So put the excess back in the pot and save it for tomorrow, unless you have just run five miles. In that case, you can eat as much as you wish. Knowing what standard servings are helps you decipher exactly what portions you should use for yourself. If you wish to lose weight, take a look at what you have been serving yourself and how much energy (calories) it is actually providing. It will say on the Nutrition Facts label. Use your food label reading know-how.

Join the slow-food movement, dedicated to "Taste, Tradition, and the Honest Pleasures of Food." SLOWFOODUSA.ORG

The Slow Food Movement

Let's consider the total environment surrounding food—the who, when, where, why, and how of eating. Create a nurturing environment around your meals. Many people are victims of the fast-food movement. We all seem to be slaves to our schedules, willingly or unwillingly, but remember, we need to stop focusing on what we are doing wrong, and focus on what we have stopped doing right. Think back a decade or two or even to your childhood. I remember sitting down to dinner with my family every night, almost always at six o'clock. We had a big antique table, and it was my job to clear off the clutter and set the plates. We almost always had a tablecloth or place mats, and often my mom had either daisies or daffodils from the yard on the center of the table, or candles or some seasonal centerpiece. My dad was a musician and soft jazz was always playing. All our meals, with rare exceptions, were prepared by loving family hands. Mostly, we used dinnertime to discuss the day, and often it took an hour or more to finish the meal. The TV was never on and the phone didn't ring much. And, of course, this was before the advent of cell phones. I don't remember, as a kid, ever eating when I wasn't hungry or overeating at the dinner table. Those were the days when families weren't running frantically in ten different directions.

TEN STEPS TO THE MEDITERRANEAN

1. Use olive oil.
2. Eat leafy green salads often.
3. Turn nuts, seeds, and fruit into your favorite snacks.
4. Generously indulge in whole grains (whole-grain breads and pasta).
5. Have legumes (anything that grows in a pod: beans, lentils, peas) several times a week.
6. Introduce two to three vegetarian meals a week.
7. If you eat animal protein, choose poultry.
8. Eat salmon, sardines, or other cold-water fish twice weekly.
9. Serve fruit for dessert.
10. Savor every morsel of food. Love your company (especially yourself). Marvel at the music. Flicker in the candlelight. Take time to smell the fresh flowers.

Times have changed, but we can still create a nurturing environment around our meals with just a bit of determination. And the idealist in us feels that it would be so wonderfully beneficial to go back to the "good old days," sit around a table at dinner, "dining" for one to two hours, relaxing, enjoying everyone and everything, including the food. It is relaxing to retire after an evening of leisurely conversation, homemade food, and genuine connection with the people who are important to us (just oneself, or family members, or friends).

Do this for yourself. Set apart a small space just for eating, even if it is just one end of a work space. Select a simple candle or flower or plant. Place beautiful plates, bowls, glasses, and flatware on a place mat or tablecloth. Play soothing background music, prepare simple, nutritious food, and serve it thoughtfully on the table. Take extra time to linger. Just think, you're already part of the slow-food movement. Yes, think about slowing down just three times during your day.

Food for Your Mood

Among those billions of cells in our bodies are many, many neurotransmitters. They are simply the chemical messengers of the brain and the body. They impact our thoughts, our emotions, and our motivation, just to mention a few of their "jobs." You can easily see how they benefit your pursuit of a healthy weight and a happy life: they can help minimize depression, shift your mood, promote calmness, and diminish mood swings; they can transmit and give more energy, create better concentration, reduce stress levels, encourage sleep, create more alertness, even diminish cravings for sweets. The four neurotransmitters are serotonin, dopamine, acetylcholine, and norepinephrine. Serotonin helps calm the mind and the body. Natural sugars, which are unrefined carbohydrates found in grains and fruits and vegetables, help stabilize mood swings and encourage the production of serotonin. Foods containing the amino acid tryptophan also help build your supply of serotonin. Tryptophan can be found in tofu, legumes (anything in a pod), avocados, whole grains, and poultry (for example, turkey may make you mellow after a big Thanksgiving dinner). Healthy levels of serotonin calm cravings for simple carbohydrates, such as cookies, cakes, pies, chips, and other highly processed snacks.

Dopamine is the neurotransmitter that moderates concentration, energy, and motivation. The amino acids tyrosine and phenylalanine support the production of dopamine and are present in fish, rice, dairy products, and eggs.

The neurotransmitter acetylcholine is responsible for memory and general mental agility. Foods containing choline will support theses functions, and include oatmeal, whole grains, sesame seeds and tahini, tofu (and tempeh and miso), nuts, and brewer's yeast.

> ## MOTIVATION MAKER
>
> *Indulge a Craving for Sweet or Salty*
>
> These foods are on the top of our list: dark chocolate, dried fruits (nature's candy), a slice of whole-grain bread with jam or honey or cinnamon sugar, or a bowl of whole-grain cereal. For that salty craving, enjoy whole-wheat bread dipped in olive oil, salt, and balsamic vinegar, or olives. This way you are still providing yourself nourishment, not empty calories.

Norepinephrine is the neurotransmitter responsible for uplifting mood, and can provide balance during stressful situations. The amino acid phenylalanine is the supporting food for this neurotransmitter. Protein sources—including poultry, eggs, fish, and legumes, in addition to beets, leafy greens, apples, and dark chocolate—will provide you with good sources of norepinephrine-boosting foods.

It's important to understand that when moodiness is plaguing you, with a bit of judicial thinking, you can easily direct your choices to foods that will change your mood for the better.

Why You Might Consider Organics

There are many chemicals that become part of our food during certain stages of plant propagation, harvesting, and animal breeding. Agrichemicals such as pesticides, herbicides, prophylactic antibiotics, and growth hormones are not good for our health. Nor are they good for the environment. It is important, ultimately, to aim for organically produced foods. Organic means that animals and crops are grown without additives such as pesticides, antibiotics, and hormones. Pesticides are used on most crops to ensure higher yield through reduced insect damage or weed control. Research indicates that there may be health risks to ingesting pesticides. It is logical to assume that pesticides could be harmful to human health to some degree if they are potent enough to kill insects, weeds, and animal pests. Some fruits and vegetables are more heavily sprayed than others. The Environmental Working Group in Washington, DC, (www.ewg.org) provides a list of the most heavily sprayed crops. The list usually includes strawberries, bell peppers (red and green), spinach, cherries, peaches, Mexican cantaloupe, celery, apples, apricots, green beans, Chilean grapes, and cucumbers. Exposure to pesticides can be reduced by 50 percent if an individual chooses to select fewer of these fruits and vegetables or to buy them organically. The use of prophylactic antibiotics and growth hormones is common in conventionally raised animals and poultry. These antibiotics and growth hormones remain in the animal, and are ultimately ingested when you buy and prepare those animal products or eat them in restaurants. They are not good for your health and do not support your healthy weight and healthy lifestyle.

> *The Journal of Applied Nutrition* reported that ounce for ounce, organic fruits and vegetables are twice as rich in certain nutrients as non-organic produce.

Water, Water Everywhere

Drink one big glass of plain water first thing in the morning. It helps you stay hydrated and flushes out toxins and the normal wastes occurring from metabolism. Throughout the rest of your day, drink plain water when you are thirsty. By eating lots of fruits and vegetables, you can get about 40 percent of the water you need from your food.

Does water suppresses the appetite? No! Although being well hydrated maintains excellent metabolism, drinking a great amount of water does not reduce the amount you eat. Water empties from the stomach very quickly. To feel full with less, eat foods that have a high water content, such as fruits, vegetables, and clear soups because they empty slower from the stomach than plain water.

Following are some examples of water content in everyday foods:

FOOD	WATER CONTENT
Lettuce	95%
Watermelon	92%
Strawberries	91%
Vegetable Soup	90%
Carrots	88%
Apples	84%
Corn	76%
Bananas	75%
Cooked Pasta	66%

BELIEF BOOSTER

Eat breakfast like a king, lunch like a prince, and dinner like a pauper.

In the morning, give the body a substantial and balanced meal to fuel the day's activities. Eat a lighter lunch, perhaps after a half-hour walk. Dinner should be very simple and light to allow for a pleasant evening reading, enjoying hobbies, or doing moderate physical activity.

Research from the National Weight Control Registry indicates that 78 percent of people who have lost weight and maintained that weight loss eat breakfast every day.

Eating Out

More Americans are eating out than ever before. Unfortunately, the restaurants are serving foods that are higher in fat and sugar (so higher in calories), in humongous portions at very low prices. Simply ban fast food. It has no place in your healthy lifestyle. Choose restaurants that serve healthy, balanced meals. Remember this combination: 60 percent complex carbohydrates (whole grains, vegetables, and fruits), 15-20 percent protein, and 20-25 percent healthy oils.

Obesity Research published a study that found that subjects ate 73 percent more when served larger portions. When eating out, share an entrée or order just appetizers or side dishes.

A few small tastes lead to gradual and lifelong changes in palate. Often, your palate only needs a week or so to become accustomed to a new fresh taste. This can mean the difference between a salty deep-dish pizza with extra cheese from the local pizza place and a whole-grain pita with fresh mozzarella, oregano, and tomatoes drizzled with olive oil. You will soon be hungry for, maybe even crave, wholesome food.

Nourishing the Rest of Yourself

We all need to indulge ourselves with special "treats," especially while making lifestyle changes. Even though these changes are good, they can still induce temporary stress. Consider the following "treats" to help ease you into your new lifestyle and perfect weight:

- Take a few minutes each day for your favorite reading. Find a private reading room in your home (a room you can actually lock if you want to) where you can spend a few uninterrupted minutes blissfully thumbing through a magazine or favorite novel.
- Learn how to knit. Knitting is a proven stress reliever, keeps the hands busy, and results in something very warm, soft, and cuddly.

- Nourish your "skin hunger." Get a massage.
- As we've suggested before, unclutter your clothes closet. Put in a cardboard box (yes, just like the pantry) all the clothes that you have not worn for a year, that do not fit, that do not have the potential to be flattering when you reach your perfect weight, or that do not delight you.
- Browse magazines for a new wardrobe. We prefer natural fibers and comfortable, loose-fitting clothing.
- We all love the aromas of delicious foods. Enlarge your aromatic knowledge and learn what natural fragrances and essential oils appeal to you (lavender, eucalyptus, cedar wood, and rosemary are our favorites).
- Take the time to enjoy and play good music.
- Find a sauna or steam room for a regular "detoxifying" relaxation.
- Silence is golden. Sequester yourself in some quiet corner of the house, or take a serene walk in a park or along a quiet road.

Breathe In, Breathe Out

Breathing is quite literally "inspiration." Deep breathing creates optimum oxygenated blood and ensures very efficient use of mind and body: from thinking to optimum physical activity. Breathe in through the nose for four counts, hold for seven counts, breathe out eight counts. Focus on the sound of your breathing. Notice how tension dissolves, stress is released, healing is facilitated, general well-being is apparent, and perfect weight is supported. Practice this breathing exercise at least twice a day, but no more than four breaths at each practice in the beginning.

Sleep: Be Still, Be Quiet, Be Tranquil, Be Calm, Be Inactive, Lie Still

As we have pointed out, recent research strongly suggests that adequate sleep promotes healthy weight and inadequate sleep

MOTIVATION MAKER

Create a Spa Day Right at Home

With just a bit of advance preparation, imagine what it would be like:

Put on a new pair of walking shoes and take a brisk walk for half an hour (starting from your front door). Come home for a plate of whole-grain toast and scrambled eggs (or similar variation). Meander into the bathroom and fill a Tupperware basin with warm, soapy water, and recline in a comfortable chair while you soak your feet for twenty minutes. Dry your feet off and give yourself a short foot massage. Spend the next two hours indulging in something new (whether a music lesson for flute, a streaming virtual yoga class, or a good book—you choose). Lunch! Be sure your plate has something "grainy," something protein, and something vegetable. An afternoon snooze (with or without a facial or a cool washcloth on your eyes) for half an hour to an hour. Mid-afternoon, another pleasant half-hour walk around the neighborhood. Late afternoon, step into the shower for a body scrub and the full deal: shampooing, shaving, nail filing and clipping. Dinner! Lots of vegetables, whole-grain bread dipped in olive oil, and a piece of fish or meat, or egg or vegetable protein (tofu, tempeh, beans, nuts, and seeds). After dinner? Watch a travel DVD and read another chapter of your book before slipping into bed between clean sheets for a full eight hours of deep, restful slumber. Remember to eliminate the "sound clutter" in your home. Turn down (or off) the ringers on your phones and unplug the TV, radio, and computer.

promotes weight gain. This seems fairly obvious. After all, when we are tired, we don't want to be active and we usually want to snack more. Additionally, in *The Promise of Sleep,* Dr. William C. Dement writes that when people are sleep deprived, the resulting lack of energy means that they don't burn as many calories as when they are rested and more active. The body reacts by saving calories as fat, making weight loss much more challenging.

Research is revealing a deeper level of understanding of this simple concept of weight gain and sleep deprivation. A study at the University of Chicago, published in an article in the October 23, 1999 issue of the British medical journal *The Lancet,* explained that there are two hormones in our bodies that regulate appetite: ghrelin and leptin. Ghrelin sets appetite into motion in humans, and this hormone was found at higher levels in people who were regularly sleep deprived. The hormone leptin signals the body when it is satisfied and should stop eating. In sleep-deprived individuals, leptin was at much lower levels.

Rubin R. Naiman, Ph.D., in his book *Healing Night,* mentions that "Americans today are sleeping an average of about seven hours per night ... and 30 percent of adults obtain six hours or less of sleep per night."

Now you ask: "How do I get a full night's sleep so my hormone levels of ghrelin and leptin support my perfect weight?" Here are ideas for more restful sleep:

- Avoid napping during the day if you have difficulty sleeping at night.
- Limit or omit the use of alcohol and caffeine, and avoid smoking, especially in the late afternoon and evening hours.
- Get regular exercise, but not within three hours of retiring for the night.

- Begin to calm your mind before bedtime by avoiding excess mental activity, which means do not read or watch TV, especially in your bed.
- Do not go to bed hungry, but also do not eat a full meal within three hours of going to sleep. Protein especially triggers the body to become active.
- Take a warm bath before bed to increase your body temperature.

IN THEIR OWN WORDS ...

Using this program, my total cholesterol dropped nearly fifty points, my triglycerides were cut in half, and I dropped twenty-one pounds. I am not dieting, but am following the dietary suggestions and listening to the CD for reinforcement and stress reduction. What I like most about this is that my three children, two in college and one a senior in high school, are adopting many of these eating recommendations as well. So now I know that they are not fated by family genetics to high cholesterol and heart disease—these are steps that work!

CATHLEEN

So sleep tight, and awaken the next morning refreshed, ready to eat well, happy, and eager to move along your path to success.

Our bodies will always be asking for favorite not-so-healthy foods and other fine pleasures, and we will inevitably indulge the "child" within us. But we must hold high in our minds that the greatest indulgences to give our bodies are invigorating exercise, wholesome foods, creative pursuits, and deep, restful slumber.

We request that you make one final wise choice. Remember the children: your children, and the children of those near and dear to you. Since 1995, the rate of obesity has doubled in children and tripled in teenagers. We need to pass on a very dear legacy to them. They need to be lovingly taught the importance of salubrity, excellent health, and what they can do to achieve it for themselves. Teach them what you *know*. Model for them what you *do*. Pass it on. It is the most important legacy and gift you can give.

One cannot think well, love well, sleep well, if one has not dined well.

VIRGINIA WOOLF,
A Room of One's Own

CHAPTER 10

NOW YOU HAVE IT

Everything you need is already within you.

I n this chapter, we would like to review the underlying concepts that we've covered throughout the book. These are the foundation of the Self-Hypnosis Diet and the reason so many clients have had success with the program. At the beginning of this book, we invited you to simply pretend like a child, relearn the delights of your youth, and explore the mind-body connection. We said that the Self-Hypnosis Diet does not impose a diet on you. Instead, it provides the *missing ingredient* in all other diets. It addresses the role and power of your mind to make any diet or lifestyle change more effective.

Now you have read many of the ideas in this book and your mind-body has absorbed them into deep memory. It does not matter whether or not you can recite all the ideas. They are there, deep within your memory, perfectly managed by your mind-body, just waiting to be activated. Have confidence in your mind and body. Your subconscious manages everything for you without having to trouble you with thinking tasks and decisions. Allow yourself to consider once again all the things it does for you every second of the day. For example, your mind-body is breathing you, inhaling and exhaling with the perfect rhythm for your needs at this very moment. Your mind-body is also regulating your heartbeat, your digestion, your immune responses, and myriad other mind-body processes. Your memory function is also managed by your subconscious, letting you forget and remember as needed throughout your day. If, upon reading an idea, you think to yourself, "I wouldn't like that," or "That's not for me," your mind-body places that idea back on the memory shelf to await your permission. The ideas about which you think, "I would love to experience that!" or "That's what I want!" your mind-body gathers from the memory shelf and brings up for you to use. The more you use an activity, the more your mind-body learns to do it automatically for you. Your self-hypnosis puts it all together for you, making your motivation, beliefs, and expectations the recipe for your mind-body to follow. Let's review the key points about self-hypnosis and weight loss. At any point in your journey to your perfect weight, you can become grounded by remembering the truths of the Self-Hypnosis Diet.

Eleven Truths about Self-Hypnosis and Weight Loss

1. **Self-hypnosis is an effective way to access your mind-body connection, and to deliver ideas and images of your perfect weight to your subconscious.** There is an abundance of clinical literature testifying to the effectiveness of hypnosis in influencing physical or mind-body functions. The studies done for various medical conditions clearly demonstrate the power and clinical effectiveness of self-hypnosis. You do not have to wait for

a hundred more studies to be published about weight loss and hypnosis. You can blaze your own trail right now. Your self-hypnosis can help you overcome obstacles and excuses by letting you choose, and subconsciously empower, the ideas, feelings, beliefs, and behaviors that will produce the results you want. It can also help you overcome obstacles and excuses by subconsciously acting upon your choices, ideas, feelings, beliefs, and behaviors that will produce the results you want.

2. **Self-hypnosis lets you use the power of belief and believing.** By focusing and directing this power within mind-body, your subconscious accepts and acts on your beliefs as true—even when they are false beliefs. It has been proven that individuals can hold a belief in mind that lets them walk over hot coals without creating a burn response. A cold object that is believed to be blisteringly hot can be touched and actually produce a burn response (a blister). You can choose what to believe and energize it with your faith or certainty of knowing it to be true for you. Your self-hypnosis lets you take advantage of the wisdom that "It is done unto you according to your faith." Your mind-body even accepts false beliefs, because it does not distinguish between what is real and what you imagine or pretend to be real. Become mindful of what you allow yourself to believe on a daily basis.

3. **Self-hypnosis lets you reframe and re-program subconscious patterns and responses so that they become consistent with your motivation, beliefs, and expectations about your perfect weight.** Many of your behavioral patterns, food preferences, and beliefs about your weight and yourself were created early in life before you had the awareness and intellectual sophistication to make choices about what was being learned in your mind-body. A good example

of this is the effect that being a *clean plate club member* has had on confusing the sensations of hunger, fullness and when to *stop* eating. Reprogramming this pattern with the belief that you do not have to clean your plate can help you clarify when to stop eating. Self-hypnosis lets you undo the subconscious learning that followed emotional and traumatic experiences. Whatever is learned can be unlearned by learning something else in its place. Your self-hypnosis provides the means to learn habits and patterns that give you the perfect weight results you want. This includes eating and hunger patterns, food preferences, the emotional relationship to foods and eating, self-image, the effect of trauma, and other subconscious dynamics affecting you.

4. **Self-hypnosis provides an array of tools (hypnotic phenomena) that can help you achieve your perfect weight.** These include: remembering and forgetting, altering sensory perception, time distortion, post-hypnotic suggestion, and more. For example, you might use your self-hypnosis to assign a wonderful taste to foods that help you achieve your perfect weight, and assign an undesirable taste to foods that work against your perfect weight. Post-hypnotic suggestions are another of the many tools or hypnotic phenomena available to you. You can hypnotically suggest that you will experience a wonderful feeling of fullness halfway through a meal and leave the remainder uneaten. Or you may distort time or forget about cravings or desires for sabotaging snacks.

5. **Self-hypnosis can alter the way you perceive obstacles to making changes in physical activity, exercise, and other behaviors that are necessary and enjoyable in achieving your perfect weight.** It does not matter if your past has not included regular patterns of physical activity and exercise. That is in the past now. Your self-hypnosis

can help you to view exercise as desirable and rewarding. It can help remove the obstacles to greater physical activity by helping you create the attitude that matches the behaviors to produce the results you desire.

6. **Self-hypnosis is a very effective way to experience the antidote to stress—relaxation.** Self-hypnosis helps lessen the stress associated with changing habits, attitudes, and behaviors, and can create an effective barrier and insulation to the ways in which stress can affect reactive eating behavior and physical function. You cannot be relaxed and anxious or stressed at the same time. They are two different physiological states. As you practice your self-hypnosis, your mind-body is memorizing the ability to produce a relaxation response. You can trigger the relaxation response when you find yourself in stressful situations that jeopardize your perfect weight. This can range from stress during holiday meals when others want you to eat massive quantities of the food they serve you, to routine work stresses that you previously calmed by eating something. You can also produce a relaxation response when you are in the midst of removing an old habit and creating a new one.

7. **Self-hypnosis can transform and redirect the strong energies of cravings and temptations into feelings and behaviors that safeguard your perfect weight.** Your practice with self-hypnosis teaches you how to selectively detach or dissociate from your environment and your inner state. This lets you remember the detached state or become a detached observer and notice that "cravings are present"—and then choose what to turn that energy into for your purposes. You do not need to try to deny cravings and temptation; instead, simply detach from the feelings they produce and observe that they are present. Your self-hypnosis is an excellent way to rehearse your ability to detach well enough to

then choose what you want to experience instead. This is also one of the ways that hypnosis is used to create hypnotically induced anesthesia.

8. **Self-hypnosis can help you create a more pleasurable and loving relationship with food, eating, and your body, making your weight loss and lifestyle changes more effective and enjoyable.** As you create and enjoy greater pleasure with new habits of eating and physical exercise, you will maintain them. A loving relationship with anything lets you enjoy your experience with it. Your self-hypnosis helps you do the inner work of loving that creates the results you want for your perfect weight.

9. **Self-hypnosis is a form of focused concentration that effectively enhances your ability to mentally rehearse achieving the results you desire.** Mental rehearsal has been used by athletes and performers for years. Studies have shown mental rehearsal to be an effective way to practice one's mind-body for the actual performance. Your self-hypnosis lets you rehearse the pleasure of your performance at special occasions, holiday dinners, and parties. You can hypnotically rehearse your food and beverage choices, your confidence in declining dishes or drinks, and satisfaction in handling the situation so very well. Rehearsing in mind, you are preparing your mind-body to serve your perfect weight and pleasure in advance.

10. **Self-hypnosis effectively enables the repetition and practice of hypnotic suggestions that result in lifelong, permanent patterns of behavior, emotion, and belief about your perfect weight. Whatever you regularly practice with your self-hypnosis will become the conscious and subconscious patterns of the lifestyle that maintains your perfect weight.** Before you know it, you will hear yourself telling others that you do not have to

think about dieting or weight loss anymore. Your lifestyle is now in action, developing the patterns and habits that produce the results you want. Your self-hypnosis paved the way for many changes while letting you concentrate on discovering and creating your very own recipe for perfect weight.

11. **The Self-Hypnosis Diet is not a diet.** It provides the *missing ingredient* that helps you use your mind-body to establish lifelong patterns of eating and exercise that make it seem like you can eat anything you want and still keep your perfect weight.

This is not the end. It is not even the beginning of the end.
But it is the end of the beginning.
WINSTON CHURCHILL

APPENDIX A

Answers to Chapter 1 Quiz

1. Hypnosis is complicated and takes many sessions and much instruction.
   FALSE. It is natural, simple, and easy.

2. To experience hypnosis, you must be hypnotized by someone who knows how to do it to you.
   FALSE. Hypnosis is not done *to* anyone *by* anyone, but a skilled therapist can teach you how to learn and use hypnosis.

3. When experiencing a hypnotic trance, one loses consciousness.
   FALSE. There is no loss of consciousness. This is one of the greatest misconceptions about hypnosis.

4. The subconscious mind cannot tell the difference between what is real and what is imagined.

TRUE. The subconscious acts upon what is imagined as real. Brain-scan studies have shown activity in the brain even when only offered suggestions to imagine.

5. Hypnosis can make you do things that are against your will or violate your values.

FALSE. While under hypnosis, you are always in control and maintain your values and morals.

6. Most people go into trance every day.

TRUE. There are many examples of everyday normal trance states, like being glued to the TV, reading a book, being absorbed in a movie or activity, or daydreaming.

7. All hypnosis is self-hypnosis.

TRUE. Absolutely true.

8. Hypnosis can help your body heal wounds faster.

TRUE. Research on hypnosis and wound healing shows that hypnosis can be used to accelerate healing of wounds and other conditions or injuries.

9. Your body has a language of its own.

TRUE. While you understand both literal and figurative speech, your body, or subconscious, understands on a literal level. So when you say someone "is a pain in the neck," your body will try to create what you have spoken by increasing muscle tension or spasm after repeated messages to yourself.

10. You can use hypnosis to influence your physical responses like digestion, breathing, etc.
    TRUE. Hypnosis helps you use your mind-body connection in order to influence many functions and systems within your body.

11. Stage hypnosis is the same as medical hypnosis.
    FALSE. Stage hypnosis is purely for entertainment, while the purpose of medical hypnosis is to help people.

12. Sometimes you are not even aware that you are already in a trance.
    TRUE. When you are absorbed with interest, you may not be paying attention to what is around you, such as when you are engrossed in a movie or a book, or a fascinating home-study course.

13. Hypnosis is a purely mental or psychological phenomenon—it is "all in the mind."
    FALSE. While this was once thought to be true, sophisticated brain scans with MRI and PET imaging equipment show that what we imagine while in trance has a physical effect within the body.

14. There are some people who cannot be hypnotized. TRUE. Individuals with serious cognitive deficit or retardation may not be able to concentrate well enough to follow instructions and become absorbed in their thoughts, ideas, or images.

15. With hypnosis, you can give messages to your body and your body can give messages to you.

TRUE. Interactive methods of hypnosis allow you to obtain information from your body about the purpose or meaning of symptoms it may be producing, as well as receive suggestions from you for healing.

16. There are thousands of published research studies and articles that demonstrate the benefits and effectiveness of hypnosis.

TRUE. *The International Journal of Clinical and Experimental Hypnosis,* published by the Society of Clinical and Experimental Hypnosis, and the *Americal Journal of Clinical Hypnosis,* published by the American Society of Clinical Hypnosis, are just two journals that have been publishing research over the past fifty years, not to mention the research printed in other professional medical and psychological journals and books.

APPENDIX B

The History of Hypnosis Timeline

2600 BC—The father of Chinese medicine, Wang Tai, taught his peers a method of healing that involved passing the hands over the patient's body while speaking words for curing.

1500 BC—Accounts can be found in the Hebrew Bible ("laying on of hands") and the Talmud of healing approaches similar to hypnosis.

1000 BC—Egyptians used healing techniques very similar to current-day hypnosis, in what they called "Sleep Temples."

400 BC—In ancient Greece, Asclepiades stroked his patients with his hands, leading them into sleeplike states in his healing temple, which he called the "abaton."

BC 460–370—Hippocrates spoke of hypnosis when he said "the affliction suffered by the body, the soul sees quite well with the eyes shut."

1493–1541—Paracelsus, Swiss physician and philosopher, believed that magnetic radiation affected the health of the human body. Thought, belief, and will were understood to affect health.

1628–1683—Valentine Greatrakes, healer in England and Ireland, manually stroked the diseased parts of patients. The concepts of belief and confidence were part of this treatment.

1734–1815—Franz Anton Mesmer (France) merged the ideas of the 1600s and 1700s into "animal magnetism." The beginning of modern hypnosis was termed "mesmerism." (Mesmer was one of the first physicians to advocate low-cost health care and the idea of traveling medical clinics.)

April 12, 1829—The first application of hypnosis as surgical anesthesia.

1836—The first tooth extraction using mesmerism.

1846—The first leg amputation using mesmerism.

Mid-1800s—James Braid, Scottish physician, borrowed the early "hypn" nomenclature from the French, using the term "hypnotism."

Mid-1800s—James Esdale, Scottish surgeon working in India, documented hundreds of cases of major surgery using hypnosis as the only anesthetic, including leg amputations and abdominal operations. It was significant that his mortality rate was only 5 percent compared with the standard 50 percent mortality rate of others without hypnosis as the anesthetic.

1836—First recorded use of hypnosis as surgical anesthesia in the United States (Boston).

1849—John Elliotson founded a mesmeric hospital. He also published the first journal dealing with hypnosis, *The Zoist*.

Late-1800s—Jean Martin Charcot, a most influential neurologist in Paris, found that hypnosis relieved nervous conditions and mental disorders.

1870s—The field of hypnosis declined due to the use of chemical anesthetics and also because of fringe practitioners, unqualified practitioners, stage entertainers, and charlatans, all of whom lowered the reputation of medical techniques of hypnosis.

1856–1939—Sigmund Freud used hypnotized people in his exploration of the unconscious state, later developing his system of psychoanalysis. He was heavily influenced by Jean Martin Charcot.

1920s—American Clark L. Hull, university professor of psychology, designed experiments to test hypnosis. He stated, "Hypnosis is a heightened form of suggestibility," and generated renewed interest in the failing trend of hypnosis.

World War I and World War II—Hypnosis was increasingly used by physicians and psychologists for shell shock (now called post-traumatic stress disorder) and other mental disorders stemming from war experiences. Also, as drugs for pain were unavailable, many physicians used hypnosis successfully.

c.1930–1980—Milton Erickson (student of Clark Hull), a prolific contributor to hypnotic treatment and a master of indirect hypnosis, was known for leading patients into trance without using the word "hypnosis." He is probably the best known twentieth-century American practitioner of medical hypnosis.

1949—The Society for Clinical and Experimental Hypnosis was founded. SCEH is an international organization of psychologists, psychiatrists, social workers, nurses, dentists, and physicians.

1950s—Herbert Spiegel described the "natural hypnotic talents of patients."

1957—The American Society of Clinical Hypnosis was founded by Milton Erickson.

1958—The AMA (American Medical Association) issued statements supporting hypnosis.

1960s—Harold Crasilneck pioneered hypnotic work with stroke patients and pain patients.

Present—Hypnosis is high on a wave of interest. Research is prevalent, and new techniques are being developed that are increasing the effective use of hypnosis in modern society.

FURTHER READING AND RESOURCES

Books

Andreas, Jamie. *The Principles of Correct Practice for Guitar.* New York: Jamey World, Inc., 2004.

Benson, Herbert. *The Relaxation Response.* New York: Avon Books, 1975.

Borysenko, Joan. *Minding the Body, Mending the Mind.* Reading, MA: Addison-Wesley Publishing Company, Inc., 1987.

Bristol, Claude M. *The Magic of Believing.* New York: Pocket Books, 1991.

Cole-Whittaker, Terry. *What You Think of Me Is None of My Business: A Dynamic Inspirational Leader Shows You How to Follow Your Own Inner Path to Happiness, Success, and Self-Fulfillment!* New York: Jove Books, 1998.

Coué, Émile. *Self Mastery Through Conscious Autosuggestion.* Whitefish, MT: Kessinger Publishing, 1997.

Crasilneck, Harold B., and James A. Hall. *Clinical Hypnosis: Principles and Applications.* 2nd ed. Orlando, FL: Grunke & Stratton, 1985.

Critser, Greg. *Fat Land: How Americans Became the Fattest People in the World.* New York: Houghton Mifflin, 2003.

Daley, Rosie, and Andrew Weil. *The Healthy Kitchen.* New York: Knopf, 2003.

Dement, William C., and Christopher Vaughan. *The Promise of Sleep: A Pioneer in Sleep Medicine Explores the Vital Connection Between Health, Happiness, and a Good Night's Sleep.* New York: Dell, 2000.

Emoto, Masaru. *The Messages from Water III.* Tokyo: Hado Kyoiku Sha Co., Ltd., 2004.

Fallon, Sally. *Nourishing Traditions: The Cookbook That Challenges Politically Correct Nutrition and the Diet Dictocrats.* 2nd ed. Winona Lake, IN: New Trends Publishing, Inc., 1999.

Guiliano, Mireille. *French Women Don't Get Fat: The Secret of Eating for Pleasure.* New York: Knopf, 2004.

Haas, Elson M. *Staying Healthy with Nutrition: The Complete Guide to Diet and Nutritional Medicine.* Berkeley, CA: Celestial Arts, 1992.

———. *Staying Healthy With the Seasons.* 21st anniv. ed. Berkeley, CA: Celestial Arts, 2003.

Hammond, D. Corydon, ed. *Handbook of Hypnotic Suggestions and Metaphors.* New York: W.W. Norton & Company, 1990.

Lipton, Bruce H. *The Biology of Belief: Unleashing the Power of Consciousness, Matter, and Miracles.* Santa Rosa, CA: Mountain of Love, 2005.

Madison, Deborah. *Local Flavors: Cooking and Eating from America's Farmers' Markets.* New York: Broadway, 2002.

Naiman, Rubin R. *Healing Night: The Science and Spirit of Sleeping, Dreaming, and Awakening*. Minneapolis: Syren Book Company, 2006.

Northrup, Christiane. *Women's Bodies, Women's Wisdom: Creating Physical and Emotional Health and Healing*. New York: Bantam, 2002.

O'Driscoll, Erin. *The Complete Book of Isometrics: The Anywhere, Anytime Fitness Book*. New York: Hatherleigh Press, 2005.

Pelletier, Kenneth R. *Sound Mind, Sound Body: A New Model for Lifelong Health*. New York: Fireside, 1995.

Pert, Candace B. *Molecules of Emotion: Why You Feel the Way You Feel*. New York: Scribner, 1997.

Robbins, John. *Diet for a New America: How Your Food Choices Affect Your Health, Happiness, and the Future of Life on Earth*. Novato, CA: H.J. Kramer, 1987.

———. *The Food Revolution: How Your Diet Can Help Save Your Life and the World*. Berkeley, CA: Conari Press, 2001.

———. *Reclaiming Our Health: Exploding the Medical Myth and Embracing the Source of True Healing*. Tiburon, CA: H.J. Kramer, 1996.

Satter, Ellyn. *Secrets of Feeding a Healthy Family*. Madison, WI: Kelcy Press, 1999.

Schlosser, Eric. *Fast Food Nation: The Dark Side of the All-American Meal*. New York: Houghton Mifflin, 2001. (excellent research on the fast-food industry)

Shomon, Mary. *The Thyroid Diet: Manage Your Metabolism for Lasting Weight Loss*. New York: Collins, 2004.

Spiegel, Herbert, and David Spiegel. *Trance and Treatment: Clinical Uses of Hypnosis*. 2nd ed. Washington, DC: American Psychiatric Publishing, Inc., 2004.

Temes, Roberta. *The Complete Idiot's Guide to Hypnosis.*
2nd ed. New York: Alpha Books, 2004.

————. *Medical Hypnosis: An Introduction and Clinical Guide.*
Oxford: Churchill Livingstone, 1999.

Travis, John W., and Regina Sara Ryan. *Wellness Workbook:*
How to Achieve Enduring Health and Vitality. 3rd ed.
Berkeley, CA: Celestial Arts, 2004.

Weil, Andrew. *Eating Well for Optimum Health: The Essential*
Guide to Food, Diet, and Nutrition. New York: Knopf,
2000.

————. *8 Weeks to Optimum Health: A Proven Program for*
Taking Full Advantage of Your Body's Natural Healing
Power. New York: Knopf, 1997.

————. *Healthy Aging: A Lifelong Guide to Your Physical and*
Spiritual Well-Being. New York: Knopf, 2005.

Weil, Andrew, and Rosie Daley. *The Healthy Kitchen.* New
York: Knopf, 2003.

Winter, Ruth. *A Consumer's Dictionary of Food Additives.*
6th ed. New York: Three Rivers Press, 2004.

Wood, Rebecca. *The New Whole Foods Encyclopedia: A*
Comprehensive Resource for Healthy Eating. New York:
Penguin, 1999. (a comprehensive guide to food)

————. *The Splendid Grain: Robust, Inspired Recipes for Grains*
With Vegetables, Fish, Poultry, Meat, and Fruit. New York:
William Morrow & Company, 1997. (a guide to grains)

Web Sites

Environmental Working Group: www.ewg.org (organics)
Dr. Steven Gurgevich and Joy Gurgevich's Web site:
www.healingwithhypnosis.com
The Slow Down Diet: www.marcdavid.com
Joyful and Competent Eating: www.ellynsatter.com

The Slow Food Movement: www.slowfoodusa.org

Dr. Weil on Healthy Aging: www.healthyaging.com

Dr. Andrew Weil's Web site: www.drweil.com

Dr. Andrew Weil's Self Healing monthly newsletter: www.drweilselfhealing.com

Gary Null's Web site: www.garynull.com (for this health and nutrition expert's excellent books, CDs, DVDs, and oher resources for natural living)

Weight-Control Information Network E-mail: win@info.niddk.nih.gov

The Surgeon General's Call to Action to Prevent and Decrease Overweight and Obesity: www.surgeongeneral.gov/topics/obesity

Magazines

Body + Soul: www.bodyandsoulmag.com

Eating Well: www.eatingwell.com

First for Women: www.firstforwomen.com

Fitness: www.fitnessmagazine.com

Food as Medicine, a special supplement to Alternative Medicine: www.alternativemedicine.com

Health: www.health.com

Men's Health: www.menshealth.com

Prevention: www.prevention.com

Science of Mind: www.scienceofmind.com

Shape: www.shape.com

Weight Watchers Magazine: www.weightwatchers.com

Yoga Journal: www.yogajournal.com

Movies and DVDs

Babette's Feast, directed by Gabriel Axel, 1987.

Big Night, directed by Campbell Scott and Stanley Tucci, 1996.

Chocolat, directed by Lasse Hallström, 2000.

Like Water for Chocolate, directed by Alfonso Arau, 1992.

Mostly Martha, directed by Sandra Nettelbeck, 2001.

Super Size Me, directed by Morgan Spurlock, 2004.

What the Bleep Do We Know!?, directed by William Arntz, Betsy Chasse, et al., 2004.

Major Professional Societies and Web Sites

American Psychological Association (APA): www.apa.org

American Society of Clinical Hypnosis (ASCH): www.asch.net

Society of Clinical and Experimental Hypnosis (SCEH): www.sceh.us

American Psychotherapy and Medical Hypnosis Association (APMHA): www.apmha.com and www.apmha.com/hypnosishelp/

(ASCH and APMHA both have a referral service on their Web sites.)

Audio CDs

Fain, Jean. *Eat to Live & Lose Weight!* Concord, MA: Jean Fain, 2005.

———. *Eating Awareness Training.* Concord, MA: Jean Fain, 2006.

———. *Mindful Eating.* Concord, MA: Jean Fain, 2005.

Gurgevich, Steven. *The Self-Hypnosis Home Study Course* (16 CDs). Boulder, CO: Sounds True, Inc., 2005.

———. *The Self-Hypnosis Diet* (3 CDs). Boulder: Sounds True, 2005.

Gurgevich, Steven and Joy Gurgevich. *Lose Weight with Hypnosis* (6 CDs), Tucson, AZ: Tranceformation Works division of Behavioral Medicine, 2002.

Pert, Candace. *Your Body Is Your Subconscious Mind.* Boulder, CO: Sounds True, 2004.

ABOUT THE AUTHORS

Steven Gurgevich, Ph.D., is a faculty member at The University of Arizona's College of Medicine, where he directs the Mind-Body Clinic and teaches mind-body medicine to physicians in Dr. Andrew Weil's Program in Integrative Medicine. He is also a fellow and faculty member of the American Society of Clinical Hypnosis. His private practice, Behavioral Medicine, Ltd. (newly named Sabino Canyon Integrative Medicine, LLC), begins its thirty-fourth year in 2007 and continues to provide Steven with valuable clinical experiences.

Now, his Web site Tranceformation.com, which includes his Healing with Hypnosis audio series, has become the newest member of the psychologist's extended professional "family," with over seventy CD titles of medical-hypnosis applications. He is the author of the 16-CD *Self-Hypnosis Home Study Course,* the 3-CD *Self-Hypnosis Diet,* and *Heal Yourself with Medical Hypnosis* with co-author Andrew Weil, M.D.

Steven is known as Dr. G. to his patients and to the

participants of the community forums on DrWeil.com and HealthyAging.com, where he serves as the mind-body expert.

Joy Gurgevich is the creator and director of The Joy of Food, her private consulting practice. She received her degree in Nutritional Sciences at The University of Arizona, where she is a nutritional consultant and preceptor for Dr. Andrew Weil's Program in Integrative Medicine. In addition, she is the behavioral nutrition expert on DrWeil.com and HealthyAging.com.

Joy's "practical training" in nutrition began over thirty-five years ago in 1969, when as a Montessori teacher, she embraced a personal and very passionate quest to use nutrition for optimizing health and well-being. Now, as a behavioral nutritionist, she teaches and guides others to achieve their goals for optimum health by eating well for body, mind, and spirit.

Joy and Steven live near Sabino Canyon National Park. Together they have five grown children; teach workshops, seminars, and practicums on "Living Well"; and tend to their organic garden and holistic home. They spend their free time walking the canyons near their home and the beach in Mazatlan, doing yoga, playing guitar, and watching DVD documentaries. Learn more about Joy and Dr. G. by visiting their Web site at www.healingwithhypnosis.com.

ABOUT SOUNDS TRUE

Sounds True was founded in 1985 with a clear vision: to disseminate spiritual wisdom. Located in Boulder, Colorado, Sounds True publishes teaching programs that are designed to educate, uplift, and inspire. With more than six hundred titles available, we work with many of the leading spiritual teachers, thinkers, healers, and visionary artists of our time.

To receive a free catalog of wisdom teachings for the inner life, please visit www.soundstrue.com, call toll-free 800-333-9185, or write: The Sounds True Catalog, P.O. Box 8010, Boulder CO 80306.

SOUNDS TRUE
awakening wisdom